Emigration from India

*The Export of Coolies,
and other Labourers, to Mauritius*

BRITISH AND FOREIGN
ANTI-SLAVERY SOCIETY

CAMBRIDGE
UNIVERSITY PRESS

CAMBRIDGE UNIVERSITY PRESS

Cambridge, New York, Melbourne, Madrid, Cape Town, Singapore,
São Paolo, Delhi, Dubai, Tokyo, Mexico City

Published in the United States of America by Cambridge University Press, New York

www.cambridge.org
Information on this title: www.cambridge.org/9781108026000

© in this compilation Cambridge University Press 2010

This edition first published 1842
This digitally printed version 2010

ISBN 978-1-108-02600-0 Paperback

EMIGRATION FROM INDIA.

THE

EXPORT OF COOLIES,

AND OTHER LABOURERS,

TO MAURITIUS.

LONDON:

THOMAS WARD & CO., 27, PATERNOSTER ROW;

AND TO BE HAD AT

THE OFFICE OF THE BRITISH AND FOREIGN ANTI-SLAVERY SOCIETY,
27, NEW BROAD STREET.

1842.

Price Sixpence.

LONDON: J. HADDON, CASTLE STREET, FINSBURY.

INTRODUCTION.

On the 12th of July, 1837, an Order in Council was issued by the government which allowed of the importation of Hill Coolies into British Guiana, under contracts for a period of five years. Availing themselves of its provisions, Messrs. Gladstone, Colville, Moss, and other proprietors of estates in that colony, introduced upwards of four hundred of these labourers, and were prepared to have introduced ten thousand more. Happily, however, for the cause of humanity, a discovery was made of the infamous means resorted to, by the agents employed in collecting these unfortunate creatures; and the utmost indignation was felt, both in British India and at home, against the continuance of such disgraceful practices. It became evident, also, that they were not confined to the case of the Coolies taken to Guiana, but that, for several years previous to the issue of the order in council, many thousands of those labourers had been, by similar means, introduced into Mauritius. Their treatment on the voyage, and subsequently to their arrival in that colony, was in keeping with the mode in which they had

A 2

been obtained in India; and finding the evils connected with the whole system incurable by any strictness of regulation or vigilance on the part of the authorities, an act prohibiting their further export was passed in India, which met with the unanimous approval of the government, the legislature, and the people of this country. Owing, however, to the extraordinary activity and influence of the agents of the Mauritian planters, Lord John Russell was prevailed upon in June, 1840, to bring forward a measure for relaxing the restrictions laid on the export of Coolies, so far as Mauritius was concerned; but his measure received a decided negative from the House of Commons, men of all parties voting against it. A large amount of official evidence, as will be seen in the following papers, has been received since that period, more fully developing the baseness of the whole affair; notwithstanding which we find that the noble lord, at present at the head of the colonial department, has introduced a measure similar in its character to that of his predecessor in office. The attention of the friends of humanity, both in and out of the House of Commons, is earnestly called to this fact, and their aid sought to defeat this new attempt to revive the Coolie-trade.

HILL COOLIES—MAURITIUS.

No. I.

From the Anti-Slavery Reporter of February 26, 1840.

WE beg to call immediate attention to the papers which have been just printed in " return to an address of the Honourable the House of Commons, dated 6th February, 1840," No. 58, relating to the Indian labourers who have been introduced into Mauritius.

This document is issued for the purpose of justifying the colonial minister, Lord John Russell, in his application to parliament to sanction an appeal to the Queen in council to relax the restrictions which were placed, a short time ago, on the export of Hill Coolies from Hindostan to any of the British emancipated colonies. It was distinctly understood at the time the restrictions were sanctioned, that they were to continue in force at least for a period of three years ; the determination of the noble lord, therefore, has come upon the British public by surprise, and has created a degree of astonishment and indignation of which, probably, his lordship is not aware.

The noble lord intends to favour Mauritius in the first instance ; British Guiana and Trinidad will, of course, in turn, enjoy the same advantage, and thus " the Gladstone slave-trade" will be revived, and British philanthropists be again compelled to remonstrate and petition against the monstrous iniquity.

The history of Mauritius is one of the blackest and foulest in the colonial annals of this country. For many years the planters of that colony prosecuted to an immense extent the slave-trade, either with the connivance, or in defiance of the authority of the executive ; and when the system of slavery was abolished by the British legislature, they had the audacity to put in their claim for compensation for upwards of 30,000 slaves who had been feloniously introduced by them into the island, and were paid the full amount of their demand without observation or remonstrance on the part of the government at home. These Mauritian planters have been, during the whole of

their connexion with this country, entirely opposed to British laws
and to British rule, and have managed by intrigue or by violence to
get rid of almost every upright and honest functionary, and to secure
to themselves and their creatures almost every office of importance
and trust; and yet these men are to be favoured with an unlimited
supply of labourers from Hindostan, and the noble lord supposes that
he will be able to secure the wretched creatures who may become
their prey from fraud and from oppression.

General Sir William Nicolay, who has been superseded in the
government of Mauritius by the appointment of Sir Lionel Smith,
was only the nominal head of the executive there : M. D'Epinay was
the real governor, and, under the management of this man in the
colony, and of Messrs. Irving and Barclay in this country, the affairs
of the island have been managed after the most approved colonial
fashion. Whether Sir Lionel Smith will be able to realize the expectations of the friends of justice and liberty in the administration
of its affairs when he arrives at Port Louis, will mainly depend upon
the fact whether he is to have a procureur general, a colonial secretary, and other important officers of his own noble principles about
him, and whether the home government will thoroughly support
him in the discharge of the high office to which he has been
appointed.

It is difficult to ascertain from the papers before us when the first
shipment of Coolies to Mauritius took place, or the exact number of
them which has been at various periods introduced. It appears that
from the 1st August, 1834, to the 24th October, 1838, there were
received from *Calcutta* 13,243 Coolies, viz., 12,994 men; 198
women; and 51 children. From the 1st June, 1837, to 22nd June,
1838, there were shipped from *Cochin* 308 Coolies, supposed to be
all males. From the 1st June, 1837, to 24th June, 1838, there were
shipped from *Pondicherry* 5058 Coolies, supposed to be all males.
From the 1st June, 1837, to the 25th August, 1838, there were
shipped from *Rajahmundry* 441 Coolies, viz., 434 men and 7 women;
making a total of 19,050—viz., 18,794 men, 205 women, and 51
children. But it is quite clear from the petition addressed to her
Majesty by the planters and others, dated 18th May, 1839, that a
much larger number of Coolies had been introduced. The 100
persons who signed that document state, that within the " last four
years" they had " caused to be brought from British India upwards
of 20,000 native Indian labourers." It is stated by some parties that
the whole number introduced cannot be much short of 30,000!

Now the first thing we want to know, is, what has been the mortality among these miserable beings during their voyage from Hindostan to Mauritius, and subsequently to their arrival there. On
both these important points, the papers before us are deficient in
information. From the crowded state, however, of most of the
vessels in which they were shipped, and the want of proper medical
attendance, we have little doubt that large numbers perished between
shipment and arrival. We find that the larger proportion of the
ships employed in the Coolie slave-trade carried from 200 to upwards

of 500 human beings each! On board two of these vessels we have an account of several suicides which took place. On board the *"Lancier"* there appears to have been five, *"malgré toutes les surveillances possibles!"* as the officers on board testify. On board the *"Indian Oak"* twelve appear to have made the attempt at various times, three only of whom perished—the other nine were saved. "June 3rd, 3 P.M., ten men jumped overboard; nine were brought back by the boats, the other missing." "June 7th, 3 P.M., a man was observed overboard swimming from the ship." Left to his fate, the captain not liking to risk the lives of the boat's crew in endeavouring to save him. "June 9th, one of the Coolies, named Dullat, reported to have fallen overboard during the night." One cannot fail to perceive in these incidents true character of the Coolie slave-trade, for we find that, notwithstanding the "eight guards" on board the *Lancier*, and the unceasing vigilance which they and the officers on board exercised, five of the Coolies, rendered desperate by their situation, destroyed themselves. With respect to the mortality which has occurred since the arrival of the Indians at Mauritius, the statements are various. It is, however, admitted by the governor to have been great, and to have been "the source of deep regret" to him. In a despatch, dated 31st Dec., 1838, the colonial secretary (Mr. Dick) thus writes:—"The mortality which has prevailed among the Indian labourers, *as well on their voyage as after their arrival here*, and more particularly on some estates and establishments, has been the source of deep regret to his excellency. Mr. Anderson, as will be seen in one of his letters appended to this communication, states the mortality of the Coolies in Port Louis" to amount to eight or nine per cent., per annum! This would be equal to the destruction of the whole number of Coolies introduced every twelve years!!

One other point deserves to be specially noticed. Out of the 19,050 Coolies introduced, of which we have any account in the papers before us, only 205 were women! It is easy to conceive, that, from this frightful disparity of the sexes, the most horrible and revolting depravity and demoralization must necessarily ensue; and that such large masses of ignorant and degraded beings must carry with them a most corrupting influence on others. We must confess that we cannot contemplate this fact without a shudder; and the most painful conviction is forced on our minds that, however immoral the negro in Mauritius was, he has been rendered more so by his contact with the Coolies.

As to the mode in which the Coolies were obtained, it is universally admitted that multitudes of them were kidnapped, and by force or fraud brought under contracts to labour in Mauritius. The "Duffadars and Crimps" have reaped a rich harvest, "notwithstanding the zealous and praiseworthy vigilance which appears to have been exercised by the officer charged with the superintendence of this branch of police duty in Calcutta, and with the execution of the ordinances passed by the supreme government on this subject." In a despatch forwarded to Lord Glenelg, dated 21st May, 1839, Sir W.

Nicolay thus writes :—"That very nefarious practices have been resorted to in many instances, in order to procure labourers for embarkation for this island, *is beyond all doubt.*" And Mr. Anderson states, that " many of them have actually been kidnapped from their own country, which they have ALL been induced to leave under circumstances of gross fraud." Will the government have the firmness and the honesty to cause a rigid and impartial inquiry to be instituted into these frauds, and give the unhappy Coolies the advantage secured to them by the order in council of the 7th September, 1838, which annuls all contracts for labour where the parties have been "induced to enter into the same by any *fraud, misapprehension, misrepresentation, or concealment ?*" This point must be urged on the government by the united voice of the people of this country.

The contracts into which the Coolies have been induced to enter are generally for five years, and the wages paid them from 3 to 5 rupees per month, and in addition 1½lbs. of rice, 4 oz. dholl, 2 to 3 oz. salt fish, 1 oz. ghee, ½ oz. salt, per diem. In some cases we perceive the allowance is rather more, and in others less. From the wages are usually deducted a rupee monthly to repay the amount expended on the voyage of the Coolies from India to Mauritius, and another rupee to repay the advances made to them previously to departure, which usually amounts to six months' pay. In addition to these deductions, a proportionate sum is withheld for absent and sick days ; and sometimes a rupee per month is retained by the employers for reconveying them back to India in case of misconduct, or, we suppose, at the termination of their period of servitude. The clothing allowed them is utterly insufficient, being scanty in quantity and coarse in quality, viz.: " 8 yards of common cloth or linen, and 2 handkerchiefs, or 2 dhooties, 1 jacket and 1 red cap per annum." The usual time of labour is from sun-rise to sun-set, with two hours relaxation for meals, except during the season of crop, which lasts six months in the year, when they are required to work as many hours as may be necessary. Now we have no hesitation in stating from experience in British Guiana, that persons held under such contracts as these are slaves ; and that such wages and allowances are utterly inadequate to sustain them in health for the performance of the heavy duties required of them in sugar cultivation.

In addition to the correspondence of General Sir William Nicolay with the home government and with the authorities in India, on the immigration of Coolies into Mauritius, the papers contain the results of an investigation into their condition by four commissioners appointed for that purpose. It appears these gentlemen examined thirty-one establishments in Port Louis, on which they found 1346 Coolies ; and twenty-two estates in the second section of the *Flacq* district, on which they found 1138 men, and 19 women. In the examination of some of the establishments in Port Louis they were assisted by Mr. Special Justice Anderson, who refused to sign the report of the commissioners for reasons which he assigns in his letters, and to which particular attention is directed. In entering upon their duties in the *Flacq* district, the commissioners met with some opposition from the planters, and, as will be seen, the governor without assigning any particular reason suddenly terminated their inquiries. But this need not be lamented, as the commissioners demonstrated that they were either incapable or unwilling, or both, to perform the duties confided to them.

OFFICIAL DOCUMENTS.

Colonial Secretary's Office, 15th October, 1838.

SIR,

1. IN pursuance of the suggestions of his Honour the President in Council at Fort William, that "the governors of the colonies to which Indian labourers have been extensively carried should be requested to appoint committees, including one or more Indian civil or military servants, or other persons who may be able to communicate personally with the labourers, and to ascertain whether they are contented with their lot, and satisfied with the manner in which the contracts with them have in general been fulfilled by the parties to whom consigned, and for whom their services were engaged," I have his excellency the governor's directions to acquaint you, that he has been pleased to select you for this duty, in which you will be assisted by the special magistrate of each section of the different districts of the island.

2. His excellency has further requested the only servants of the East India Company known to be now here, viz. Captain Forbes and Mr. T. Hugon, to associate themselves with you and the special justices, and to form a committee for this purpose.

3. The object of this inquiry being to obtain such accurate information with respect to the treatment of the Indian labourers in this colony as may tend to satisfy the government and the public of India as to their real state and condition here, it will be requisite that you should, in conjunction with the other members of the committee, visit the several establishments and estates in the town of Port Louis, and in the country districts, on which Indian labourers are employed ; and that you should, by personal communication with the Indians, endeavour to ascertain their real sentiments and feelings on the following points :—

Whether they are satisfied with the manner in which their employers, or those acting under the orders of their employers, have fulfilled the engagements entered into with the Indians.

Whether they are satisfied as to the quantity, quality, and description of the food provided for them by their employers ; the regular payment of the stipulated amount of their wages ; the hours of labour ; and, generally, with their mode of treatment.

You will also ascertain from their masters, what arrangements have been made by them for the faithful execution of that part of the engagement under which the Indians are entitled to a free passage back to their own country upon the expiration of their contract, or from inability to work through sickness, accident, or other cause.

4. On these and many other points which may suggest themselves to the committee, as tending to establish the real state and condition of the Indian labourers in this colony, it is desirable that the most accurate information should be obtained; and to assist the committee in that respect, I have the honour to enclose a copy of the injunctions laid upon all persons who obtain permission from this government to introduce Indian labourers, and of the rules established in Bengal for the grant of permits there.

5. It will be your duty to explain to the Indians the rights and privileges which they possess as free subjects in this colony, and the course they have to pursue to obtain redress if aggrieved. And it being desirable that the employers should be

present when this is done, you will be pleased to make a communication to them to that effect previously to entering into the explanation with the Indians.

6. It is further advisable, that you should take every opportunity which may occur in the course of this duty, to impress upon the Indians the expediency of depositing their money in the savings' bank, as there is but too much reason to apprehend, that in several instances crimes have been committed from a knowledge among their comrades of their carrying their money about their persons, as is the practice in India. I have, &c.

(Signed)   G. F. Dick, Colonial Secretary.

Mr. Special Justice *Campbell.*

Port Louis, 13th November, 1838.

Sir,—We have the honour to forward, for submission to his excellency the governor, our proceedings up to the 7th instant, which complete our investigation of thirty-one establishments in Port Louis.

1. We beg to state that the committee thought it unnecessary to visit those places where a less number than ten Indians were employed, as such could only be considered in the light of domestic servants.

2. The abstract of the proceedings will show where some interference may be necessary, with regard to the accommodation, medical treatment, and time allowed to the Indians for their meals.

3. Any further remarks at the present stage of our inquiry would be premature; we cannot, however, but express the hope, that in the plantations we may meet with as few exceptions to the general good treatment of the Indian labourers as have hitherto come under the observation of the committee. We have, &c.

(Signed)   C. M. Campbell.
                                             T. Hugon.
                                             J. Villiers Forbes.
                                             W. Bury.

The Honourable *G. F. Dick,* Colonial Secretary.

[*Note.*—The abstracts of evidence which accompany this letter are extremely meagre, and altogether insufficient to afford the means of a correct judgment on the actual condition of the Coolies. When their complaints are noticed we find them to be—" interference with their prejudices regarding cooking," a point of material importance in the estimation of Hindoos;—"insufficiency of time allowed for meals" —" dissatisfaction with their work "—" insufficient accommodations "—" dissatisfaction as to their food "—" want of proper medical attendance "—maltreatment by beating, &c., and non-receipt of money due to them, &c., &c. In transmitting the minutes of evidence home, the governor states, " with respect to some of them at Port Louis, there was a considerable difference of opinion between Special Justice Anderson and the other members, as to the treatment which the labourers had received from their employers, and *which does certainly not appear to have been sufficiently noticed."* This speaks volumes as to the worthlessness of the reports transmitted to him. (Vide Despatch, dated 21st May, 1839.) In calling the attention of the commissioners to this difference of opinion, in a letter addressed to them the 31st December, 1838, the Colonial Secretary (Mr. Dick) says, " The Governor trusts that in your future proceedings, you will perceive the necessity of *fully* entering into such inquiries, and of eliciting *all the facts* in similar cases, in order to leave no doubt or question with regard to them." This, however, was not done, as the abstract of their proceedings in the Flacq district fully proves.]

Colonial Secretary's Office, 17th Nov., 1838.

Gentlemen,—His excellency the governor directs me to acknowledge the receipt of your letter of the 13th inst., giving cover to the evidence taken by you with regard to the Indians employed in Port Louis, in the different establishments therein named; and as he does not perceive the signature of Mr. Special Justice

Anderson, either to the letter or the abstract of evidence, his excellency wishes to
know whether it was withheld designedly, and, if so, on what account.

I have, &c.

(Signed) G. F. DICK, Colonial Secretary.

To the Committee of Inquiry on the Indian Labourers.

Office of the Committee on Indian Labourers, Port Louis, Nov. 19, 1838.

SIR,—We have the honour to acknowledge the receipt of your letter of the 13th
inst., and beg to state that Mr. Special Justice Anderson declined signing our letter
of the 13th inst., because it did not touch upon certain general points on which his
opinions were fixed, whereas we considered, at this early stage of our proceeding,
that the expression of any such opinions would have been premature.

Mr. Anderson having signed the proceedings, his objections to signing the
abstract and letter he will fully detail in his reply to the duplicate of the letter now
under acknowledgment. We have, &c.

(Signed) C. M. CAMPBELL,
J. VILLIERS FORBES.
T. HUGON.
W. BURY.

The Honourable the Colonial Secretary.

Special Magistrates' Office, Port Louis, 19th November, 1838.

SIR,—The governor having been pleased, through your letter of the 17th inst.,
to communicate to "the Committee of Inquiry on Indian Labourers," that his
excellency had remarked the absence of my signature to the letter and the abstract
of evidence with regard to the Indians employed in Port Louis, which were addressed to you by the committee on the 13th inst., and to express a desire to be
informed if my signature was designedly withheld, and, if so, on what account, I
have the honour to state, for his excellency's information, that my signature was
intentionally withheld for the reasons which I now beg leave to submit.

As the means of facilitating reference to such a mass of papers, I fully approved
of the principle on which the abstract of evidence was adopted. It was drawn up,
however, in a manner which not only did not express the opinions which I had
formed on the evidence which had been received by the committee, but which
appeared to me to be at variance with that evidence, and calculated to mislead any
person who might have recourse to the abstract for the purpose of forming a judgment on the question at issue; under these impressions I could not feel justified in
signing such a document.

To the 4th paragraph of the letter of the 13th I could not subscribe, because I
had avowed my decided opposition to the opinions which it expresses, instead of
considering that "further remarks would have been premature," on an inquiry
which was completed with respect to Port Louis. I communicated to the committee my anxious desire that his excellency should immediately be made
acquainted with the detailed opinion of its members on the general state and condition of the Indian labourers in the town, where, as one of the committee, I
regret to say that I could discover nothing to warrant the conclusion which might
be drawn from the expression with which the letter of the 13th inst. terminates, as
I had seen much which in my opinion required immediate remedy, and merited
marked reprobation.

During the discussions which took place in the committee, it did not appear to
me that my opinion differed materially from that of the majority of its members;
but as their letter to you of the 13th induces me now to suppose that I must have
been mistaken in this respect, his excellency will perhaps expect to receive from
me the general conclusions at which I have arrived, from what I have personally
heard and seen during the progress of the inquiry, and I shall now proceed to
submit them in as few words as possible.

In a report on the state and condition of the Indian labourers in Port Louis, which, as a special magistate, I was directed to make to his excellency in the month of January last, I stated my incompetence to fulfil that duty in a satisfactory manner with the means which were then within my reach, and my report was made from the best general information which I could procure.

The power of minute investigation, with the assistance of interpreters, which has been vested in the present committee, has afforded ample means of forming a correct judgment, and its result has convinced me that the Indian labourers employed in this town are generally fed, clothed, and paid with but little deviation from their agreements. With a few exceptions, however, they are treated with great and unjust severity, by over-work, and by personal chastisement; their lodging accommodation is either too confined and disgustingly filthy, or none is provided for them; and in cases of sickness, the most culpable neglect is evinced in withholding the accommodation, the advice, and the attendance which the utter helplessness of the sufferers so urgently requires. From the various periods at which different bands have arrived, even on the same establishment, it would require considerable time and labour to make a correct calculation of the proportion of deaths annually; but I am inclined to believe that they would be found to amount to eight or nine per cent. None of the establishments in Port Louis have sufficient hospital accommodation for their sick, and the expense of placing them in the public hospital will always be offered as an excuse by the employers for not having recourse to it; but I am convinced that it is there, and there only, that serious complaints can meet with the necessary care and attention.

In most of the establishments little or no importance is attached to indulging the prejudices and customs to which Indians are known to cling so tenaciously. Their deplorable state of destitution in their own country is always advanced as an argument in favour of their improved condition here, without any reference to the change which takes place by their emigration, from comparative idleness and indolence, with the full enjoyment of all their natural prejudices, to severe and unremitting labour under many painful restrictions.

Many of them have actually been kidnapped from their own country, which they have all been induced to leave under circumstances of gross fraud; and it is a source of astonishment to me that any body of freemen, whatever may have been their former condition, should have borne, with the patience and forbearance which the Indian labourers at Port Louis have displayed, the bitter disappointment which must have attended their introduction into this island.

To induce them to come here, their ignorance is worked upon in India by the most false and deceitful representations; and the robbery and pillage which has been practised upon them in Calcutta would scarcely be credited, if the fact was not established by the most convincing testimony. They reach this colony after having been robbed of six months' pay, which is advanced in India; and when here their comfort is in every way neglected, while they are compelled, by the engagements to which their own ignorance and the avarice of others have bound them, to toil during five years for a recompence bearing no proportion to the work to which they are subjected, when compared with the common estimation of the value of labour in this colony, or to the sum which they would earn if they had the free disposal of their own time.

The harsh treatment which has been adopted or permitted by many of the employers cannot in any shape be justified in itself, and when added to the other objectionable parts of the present system, must show the necessity of applying a sure and speedy remedy, if free labour is to be placed on that footing which sound policy, justice, and common humanity would dictate. I have, &c.

(Signed)   C. ANDERSON,
                                        Superintending Special Magistrate.
The Honourable the Colonial Secretary.

———

Colonial Secretary's Office, 29th November, 1838.

SIR,—1. I have laid before the governor your letter of the 19th instant; and, with reference to the following extracts from it, I am directed by his excellency to request that you will specify the circumstances which have led you to the conclusions there stated.

13

" With few exceptions, however, they are treated with great and unjust severity,
by over-work and by personal chastisement; their lodging accommodation is either
too confined, and disgustingly filthy, or none is provided for them; and in cases of
sickness the most culpable neglect is evinced, in witfiholding the accommodation,
the advice, and the attendance which the utter helplessness of the sufferers so
urgently requires."

" In most of the establishments little or no importance is attached to indulging the prejudices and customs to which Indians are known to cling so
tenaciously."

" The harsh treatment which has been adopted or permitted by many of the
employers cannot in any shape be justified in itself, and when added to the other
objectionable parts of the present system, must show the necessity of applying a
sure and speedy remedy, if free labour is to be placed on that footing which sound
policy, justice, and common humanity would dictate."

2. The governor wishes also that you would report what you have seen which
you conceive requires immediate remedy and marked reprobation.

I have, &c.

(Signed)   G. F. DICK, Colonial Secretary.
To C. ANDERSON, Esq., Superintending Special Justice.

Special Magistrates' Office, Port Louis, 30th Nov., 1838.

SIR,—In compliance with the wishes of the governor, communicated to me by
your letter of the 29th instant, I have now the honour to state the circumstances
which have led to the conclusions on the state of Indian labourers submitted to his
excellency in my letter to you of the 19th instant; and for the sake of perspicuity,
I will deal with the subjects of objection in the order in which that letter presents
them.

Over-work.—At all the establishments where the employment is that of carters
and porters, the work commences at sunrise, and, with the exception of a very
limited interval for breakfast, is continued generally without other intermission
until dark, and often for several hours by moonlight. I myself have frequently
seen bands of Indians driving wood and rice at ten o'clock at night, and many of
them complained to the committee that they had not sufficient time to eat their
meals, and that their work was too severe.

The non-prædial apprentices who are employed in similar occupations cannot be
worked without their own consent during more than nine hours daily, while the
Indian carters and porters are compelled to labour for fourteen to fifteen hours,
and that without any sustenance after their breakfast until they retire for the night,
however late the hour may be. The proprietors of establishments of this description assert that their work is uncertain, and requires great periodical exertion; but
I cannot admit that excuse for the system which I have thought it necessary to
condemn, and which must prove injurious to the health of men so little accustomed
to severe bodily exertion as the Indians who come here are admitted to be.

Personal Chastisement.—The complaints of this nature to the committee, if my
memory is correct, were chiefly confined to the establishments of Mr. F. Berger,
Messrs. Tayler and Tyack, and Messrs. Giquel and Co.; but it is a matter of public
notoriety, that the system is carried to a great extent at Messrs. Worthington and
Co.'s, and elsewhere. This may be ascertained by a reference to the juge de paix.
On the establishment of Mr. Worthington, the proprietor vehemently objected to
its being communicated by the committee to the Indians how they were to apply
for redress when they were beaten by their masters, although there was no objection
to a similar communication for all other objects. The complaints against Mr.
Berger and Messrs. Tyack and Co. were loud and strong, and in the establishment
of the former, convincing marks of most severe stripes were exhibited to the committee by several individuals. Mr. Berger met this by threatening the complainants in the presence of the committee; and Mr. Tyack stated, that he left all the
management of the Indians in his employment to his servants.

When it was communicated to Mr. Giquel by the committee that his Indians
complained of being beaten by the person under whose immediate direction they
were, he instantly discharged him.

Knowing, as three of the members of the committee did, what takes place in Mr. Worthington's establishment with reference to bodily correction, there was some surprise expressed that it had not been alluded to by the Indians. I confess that I attributed their silence to intimidation, and I proposed, with a view to avoid this in our subsequent proceedings, that our questions should be put to the Indians when free from that restraint which, in the case of apprentices, is always felt in the presence of their master. But this suggestion was overruled; and, in my opinion, the only means of producing in the written evidence the full extent of the information which the committee was employed to search for, was consequently abandoned.

Lodging Accommodation.—On this head, my observations will be of a very general nature, for I am compelled to state, that I only saw on two establishments (Mr. Wilson's and Messrs. Watson and Co.'s), any sleeping-place which I could consider fit for the purpose to which it is devoted.

I did not expect to see separate rooms allotted to each individual, but I think they have a right to expect sufficient space and protection from the weather, accompanied by the free circulation of air, and that attention to cleanliness without which health cannot be preserved.

In no instance have the Indians in Port Louis, so far as I have seen, any thing but the bare floor provided for them; and they are generally crowded together in places where respiration would be thought almost impossible in such a climate, particularly when surrounded by the filth which invariably attends them, with the exception of the two establishments which I have mentioned. At Mr. Berger's and Mr. Lesur's, the sleeping-places are over the stable of the mules, where there is an accumulated mass of filth of every description, from which the smell above was so offensive, that I could not remain in the sleeping-loft for five minutes without suffering most disagreeably, and the inconceivably dirty state of the lofts themselves added considerably to this sensation. Messrs. Tayler and Tyack declared that they had no sleeping-place for their Indians, who are therefore obliged to have recourse to a stable or a verandah during the night.

Accommodation of and Attendance on the Sick.—The hospitals on the establishments which I have seen, are generally more calculated to increase disease than to alleviate its sufferings; and I think some of them cannot be visited by an impartial observer without exacting from him the observation, that they are unfit for the reception of human beings.

From a place of this description, an Indian was brought before the committee by his comrades in such a state of attenuation as to have become a perfect skeleton; he could not stand without the assistance of three men, and, although he had been for weeks in this state, his companions declared that he had neither received medical advice, nor any kind of attention. It is true that the master denied this, and asserted that a medical man occasionally attended his establishment; but he had no journal to produce, or any thing else to corroborate his statement. On another establishment, a man, evidently suffering under severe disease, presented himself to the committee to complain that he had been compelled to work for two months when he could hardly walk; and the employer admitted that he had neither an hospital nor a medical attendant for his establishment, and that he had considered the man's illness as a mere pretence for idleness.

Prejudices and Customs of the Indians—Much of the comfort and happiness of an Indian depends on the unrestrained pursuit of the prejudices in which he has been brought up, and the employer who attends to this feeling will benefit by his prudence, while he who neglects it will certainly suffer from complaint and discontent.

This was strongly manifested in an establishment where, in other respects, the Indians were very well treated; but, in consequence of a desire to give them food which differed from that provided by their agreement, and their cooking-place being the same as that used by the apprentices, they became very much discontented.

After what I have stated in this and in my previous letter, I cannot help again expressing my firm conviction that the state of the Indians requires some immediate regulations to protect them from over-work, to provide them with proper accommodation, and to secure to them that attention in sickness, and to their general comfort, from which the employers and their servants would reap a mutual benefit, but which I believe to be neglected in a degree which I must continue to consider highly culpable.

I have, &c.

(Signed)   C. ANDERSON,
Superintending Special Magistrate.

The Honourable the Colonial Secretary.

The Committee of Inquiry on Indian Labourers.

GENTLEMEN,   Colonial Secretary's Office, 1st December, 1838.

WITH reference to the communication made to you on the 17th ultimo, I have received his excellency the governor's directions to forward to you the explanations furnished by Mr. Special Justice Anderson for declining to sign the summary of evidence forwarded in your letter of the 13th ultimo, for any observations which you may find these explanations to require, where they are at variance with the evidence transmitted by you.

I have, &c.

(Signed)   G. F. DICK, Colonial Secretary.

The Honourable G. F. DICK, Colonial Secretary.

SIR,   Port Louis, 5th December, 1838.

1. WE have the honour to acknowledge the receipt of your letter of the 1st instant, with its enclosures (two letters from Mr. Special Justice Anderson, under date the 19th and 30th ult., in explanation of his declining to sign the summary of evidence forwarded in our letter of the 13th ult.), requiring us to make any observations, where his explanations are at variance with the evidence transmitted by us, and signed by him and the other members of the committee. We accordingly beg to submit to his excellency the governor the following observations.

2. In the second paragraph of Mr. Anderson's letter, he remarks that " the abstract was drawn up in a manner which not only did not express the opinions which he had formed on the evidence which had been received by the committee, but appeared to him to be at variance with that evidence, and calculated to mislead," &c. We beg to remark, that the abstract from the proceedings was drawn up with a view merely to facilitate reference to them, and not to express the opinions of the committee; it cannot be a matter of surprise, therefore, that Mr. Anderson did not find his opinions expressed therein, although he signed the proceedings *en masse* from which the abstract was made; a reference to the same will show whether " the abstract be at variance with the proceedings, and calculated to mislead," or not. We beg to state, that after a careful examination of both documents, we do not find any discrepancy, and are at a loss to conceive how Mr. Anderson could feel justified in signing the one document, and refusing to sign the other.

3. With respect to paragraph 3, wherein he remarks that he had " seen much which, in his opinion, required immediate remedy, and merited marked reprobation," we will merely observe that, as he did visit with the committee only 12 out of 31 establishments (other duties requiring his presence elsewhere), his opinion cannot in any way be said to result from the whole of the evidence obtained by the committee, but from other sources of information.

4. With reference to that part of paragraph 6, wherein Mr. Anderson, from his personal inspection of 12 establishments only, arrives at such a sweeping conclusion as his remark conveys, " that, with few exceptions, the Indians are treated with great and unjust severity, by over-work, and personal chastisement," &c., we cannot refrain from observing, that the only establishments seen by him with the committee wherein the remarks in any way apply, were, Messrs. Berger's, Tayler and Tyack's, and Giquel and Co.'s, to which establishments our letter of the 13th November called the attention of government. We could not, therefore, without injustice to the other establishments, coincide in opinion with Mr. Anderson in his general view of the case.

5. It is remarked, in the seventh paragraph, that, in most of the establishments, "little or no importance is attached to indulging the prejudices and customs to which Indians are known to cling so tenaciously." We would beg to observe, that in one establishment alone, viz., Mr. Diore's, did the Indians make any complaint of the kind. We are at a loss to conceive how one solitary exception can justify such a general assertion.

6. We can neither deny nor admit the fact of " kidnapping, fraud, and deceitful representation," stated by Mr. Anderson, in the eighth and ninth paragraphs of his letter, to have been employed in bringing Indians to the Mauritius, as most of the questions put to them by the committee had reference only to their treatment and feelings since their arrival; nothing, however, in the evidence received, could lead any unbiassed mind to the same conclusion as Mr. Anderson has arrived at. Only one man at Messrs. Watson and Co.'s expressed himself in a way to support the statement made of "bitter disappointment" being general; the man was a massaljee, or torch-bearer, who had evidently misunderstood the purpose for which his services were engaged. We noticed in the proceedings, that the complaint of having been plundered of their six months' advances was made by the Bengal men only.

7. Although the pay of Indians is below the present rate of town wages, most of them expressed themselves as satisfied. We doubt the disproportion being so great as implied, when the expense of their introduction is taken into consideration; for we saw in one establishment (Mr. Des Etangs') 29 men from Bombay, originally introduced by Mr. Bickajee in 1831 and 1832, who have twice voluntarily entered into new contracts, at eight rupees a month in the first instance, and 10 rupees in the second. Eleven other men, introduced by Mr. Lafauche from Bengal, had formed new engagements with Mr. Des Etangs, at the rate of 10 rupees per month.

8. We agree perfectly with Mr. Anderson, as to the unjustifiableness of harsh treatment to Indians, but we are of opinion that he is not borne out by the evidence we received, in his assertion of its "being adopted or permitted by many of the employers."

9. We now proceed to make a few observations on Mr. Anderson's letter of the 30th ult., and will endeavour to point out where his remarks are not supported by the evidence taken by the committee; we will, as much as possible, follow the same order as therein observed.

10. *Over-work.*—There were only three establishments in which any complaints at all were made with regard to the duration of work, viz., Messrs. Berger's, Tayler and Tyack's, and Duclos'. The readiness with which the men complained in that respect at Mr. Berger's, showed that they did not consider themselves bound to work after sunset, and that they thoroughly understood that part of the agreement which fixes the hours of labour from sunrise to sunset, with an intermission of three hours for meals. From our knowledge of the character of the natives, we are confident that they could not be forced to work beyond the stipulated hours without due compensation, either in money or immunity from labour at other hours during the day; the assertion of their being "compelled to work for 14 or 15 hours," is at complete variance with the declaration of the Indians themselves, with the few exceptions recorded in the proceedings.

11. *Personal Chastisement.*—We have already recorded, that some of the Indians on the three establishments alluded to by Mr. Anderson, complained of personal chastisement; but it was only at Mr. Berger's (where general discontent existed) that two men showed marks of stripes on their thighs. An allusion is made to the establishment of Mr. Worthington, as one on which personal chastisement, carried to a great extent, had long been notorious. We can say nothing of the previous existence of such an abuse on that establishment, and can only infer its having been discontinued or repressed from the evidence we received. Complaints were made about the quantity of food, which showed that the men were not intimidated by the presence of their employers.

12. The instructions conveyed to the committee would have precluded the adoption of Mr. Anderson's suggestion of examining the Indians out of the presence of the employers, had not all the other members of the committee (from their practi-

cal knowledge of the natives of India) been convinced that such a course would have been, not only invidious in itself, but totally unnecessary. There is no similitude in the position of the Indian and that of the apprentice; the latter cannot but feel restraint in the presence of the individual whose property he was but yesterday; that the former does not entertain the same feeling was amply illustrated by the complaints made in presence of the employers, trifling and frivolous in some establishments, but " loud and strong" in two, as noticed by Mr. Anderson himself. The mutual recriminations, which took place between Mr. Berger and his men, ought to have been sufficient to have convinced an unbiassed mind, that the presence of the employer did not place the Indian under any restraint in the expression of his feelings.

13. *Lodging Accommodation.*—With regard to the accommodation provided for the Indians, a reference to the proceedings will show that Mr. Anderson, in his remarks under that head, has generalized the exceptions; in very few establishments has the committee found a wilful neglect of the comforts of the Indians; in some they had so lately arrived that there had not been time to make suitable arrangements. It would be unfair to tax the employers with the filthy habits of their servants. Had Mr. Anderson ever visited India, he would not have cited as a hardship their having to repose on the " bare floor," as it is consonant to their habits; even rich natives are accustomed to sleep on a mat spread on the mud floors in the verandahs, or on the flat roofs of their houses.

14. *Accommodation of and Attendance on the Sick.*—We beg to differ in opinion with Mr. Anderson, in regard to the places set apart for the sick on the different establishments: with the few exceptions already specified, we found them sufficient for the purpose. We must confess that, in some of them, cleanliness was not strictly attended to. The excited feelings of dissatisfaction evinced by Mr. Berger's men from the beginning, induced them to bring out of the hospital, supported by two or three men, the sick man alluded to, evidently with the intent of aggravating their grounds of complaint against their employer, who assured the committee that his establishment was regularly attended by Dr. Salesse and a native doctor. Any doubt of the veracity of Mr. Berger could easily be cleared by a reference to Dr. Salesse. With regard to the other case, at Messrs. Tayler and Tyack's, there certainly was carelessness, and it was recorded on the proceedings.

15. *Prejudices and Customs.*—It is unnecessary for us to make any further remarks, as we have already touched on this subject in paragraph 5.

16. We will, in conclusion, refer to the proceedings themselves for further proof of the generalization of isolated facts which is shown in the two letters under reply; we have no hesitation in again asserting, that, from what the committee have seen in Port Louis, we could not do otherwise than report favourably on the general question, were we called upon to do so without further investigation and experience.

We have, &c.,

(Signed)   C. M. CAMPBELL.
            J. VILLIERS FORBES.
            J. HUGON.
            W. BURY.

[*Note.*—It will be clearly seen, that the attempt of the commissioners to reply to the statements in Mr. Anderson's letter, is a most impotent affair. Their abstract of the evidence, they admit, was *not* intended " to express the opinions of the committee." The third paragraph in their letter is a mere quibble; they do not deny that in the twelve establishments visited by Mr. Anderson, in company with themselves, they had " seen much" that " required *immediate remedy*, and merited *marked reprobation ;*" but they say Mr. Anderson did not visit the whole of the establishments with them, and would, therefore, have us believe, that he was not entitled to form a judgment on those he had seen. The " other sources of information" open to Mr. Anderson, might have enabled him to form a much more accurate estimate of the condition of the Coolies than that of the gentlemen honoured with the commission. In reference to the " personal chastisement" inflicted on

B

the Coolies on certain establishments which they visited, the commissioners state, that they called the attention of the government to that point in their letter of the 13th November, 1838. Not one word is said upon the subject in that letter ! On the subject of "kidnapping, fraud, and deceitful representation," they profess not to have taken evidence, and therefore, "neither deny nor admit the fact." A careful review of the evidence taken, and the *animus* of this letter, prove that they limited their inquiries within the narrowest possible range, and were unfitted for the discharge of the duties imposed upon them. It must not be forgotten, that these gentlemen resisted the proposition of Mr. Anderson to examine the Coolies apart from the presence of their masters !]

Colonial Secretary's Office, 31st December, 1838.

GENTLEMEN,—1. I have had the honour to lay before the governor your letter of the 5th instant, in answer to the observations of Mr. Special Justice Anderson, in regard to the report of the committee appointed to inquire into the state and condition of the Indian labourers here, with respect to those in Port Louis.

2. The manner in which Mr. Anderson's statement, that the prevalence of personal chastisement in the establishment of Messrs. Worthington and Co. was matter of public notoriety, and known to three members of the committee, has been noticed, is not, in his excellency's opinion, satisfactory; and he thinks that, with such information in their possession, the investigation of the committee into the existence of such an abuse should have been full and searching.

3. The third paragraph of your letter of the 13th of November did intimate that some interference might be necessary with regard to the accommodation, medical treatment, and time allowed for meals, but in terms not sufficiently strong to mark the necessity of such interference, as shown by Mr. Anderson's letters and your answer; and the governor trusts that, in your future proceedings, you will perceive the necessity of fully entering into such inquiries, and of eliciting all the facts in similar cases, in order to have no doubt or question with regard to them.

4. His excellency is disposed to be satisfied in much of the explanation you have afforded in answer to Mr. Anderson's statements, and to consider that that gentleman may have generalized too much, and may have derived his information from other sources than the evidence given before the committee; but his excellency quite concurs with Mr. Anderson in thinking that the criterion of comfort and convenience for the Indians should be taken from those of their own class in this island, and not from what they may have been used to in their own country.

I have, &c.

(Signed) G. F. DICK, Colonial Secretary.

Messrs. CAMPBELL, FORBES, BURY, and HUGON.

Colonial Secretary's Office, 31st Dec. 1838.

GENTLEMEN,—1. I have had the honour to lay before his excellency the governor, the report of your proceedings in the inquiry into the state and condition of the Indian labourers employed in the town of Port Louis; and I have received his excellency's directions to intimate to you his approval of the series of questions you have put to the Indians, as well as to the masters; but he thinks that the committee should not limit themselves to these questions, but extend them, as occasion may require, to others calculated to elucidate the real situation of these people in the different establishments in which they work, which his excellency is most desirous of having very fully ascertained.

2. For this purpose the governor requests that, in the prosecution of your inquiries in the country districts, you will be careful to note down in full detail, the whole of the evidence which is calculated in any way to establish clearly and satisfactorily the condition and state of the Indians upon the different estates and establishments.

3. The lodging accommodation afforded to the Indian labourers by their respective employers being a point on which their health and comfort are essentially dependent, his excellency is desirous that the committee should particularly inquire

into the manner in which they are lodged on the different habitations, and that your report thereon should be full and particular.

4. The mortality which has prevailed among the Indian labourers, as well on the voyage as after their arrival here, and more particularly upon some estates and establishments, has been the source of deep regret to his excellency, and renders it necessary that your inquiries should be most minute as to the medical aid and hospital treatment afforded to them by their respective employers. You will be pleased, therefore, carefully to register the name of the medical attendant of each estate, and the number of his periodical visits, as well as in describing the hospital accommodation provided for the sick. And you will, as far as may be in your power, take care to ascertain whether medical assistance to the sick is timely afforded; endeavouring to impress upon the master, that, in the medical treatment of Indians, much depends on that treatment being timely administered.

5. It should be an object of your inquiry also, to ascertain whether the Indian labourers are not employed on work of a severer description than that which they have, under their agreements, engaged to perform, and whether their hours of work are not prolonged beyond what may fairly and reasonably be expected by their employers under those engagements.

6. It will be desirable that you should note the conditions of the several agreements in a summary way, so that they may easily be compared with each other, and their various discrepancies stated, with a view to their being remedied by the adoption of some general system hereafter; and also the hours of work on each estate, in order to the introduction of some regulations to establish uniformity in that respect. Moreover, you should apprise the masters, as well as the men themselves, that, unless in cases of urgency or necessity, Sunday labour is not legal, whatever stipulation there may be in their agreements to the contrary.

7. Your inquiries should further be directed very particularly to ascertaining whether the Indians are subject to personal restraint, or other punishment or maltreatment, on the part either of their masters or of those employed under them.

I have, &c.

(Signed)   G. F. Dick, Colonial Secretary.

The Committee of Inquiry on the Indian Labourers.

Colonial Secretary's Office, 28th February, 1839.

Sir,—Having laid before his excellency the governor your letter of the 18th instant, transmitting the protest of the principal inhabitants of the first section of the Flacq District, against the manner in which the inquiry into the state and condition of the Indian labourers is conducted, I have been directed to express his excellency's regret at a proceeding on the part of the inhabitants so calculated to produce an unfavourable impression elsewhere, and to intimate to you that his excellency considers it advisable that the inquiries of the committee should cease as soon as they shall have completed the examination on those estates in the Flacq District where no opposition may be made by the proprietors.

I have, &c.

(Signed)   George F. Dick, Colonial Secretary.

To C. M. Campbell, Esq., President of the
    Committee of Inquiry on Indians.

Flacq, 16th March, 1839.

Sir,—1. We have the honour to forward, for submission to his excellency the governor, our proceedings up to the 12th instant, comprising the inquiry we have made into the state and condition of the Indian labourers on twenty-two estates on this district.

2. We have found on every estate proper accommodation for the labourers, with an hospital proportionate to the number employed (with one exception, Mr. Fabre's estate). There are four doctors in the district, who visit the estates two or three times a week, and, in case of emergency, the attendance of one of them can almost everywhere be commanded in two hours.

3. The general physical condition and health of the Indians, on all the plantations, appeared most satisfactory; the change of climate has greatly improved their constitutions. The superiority of the " huwa parree," or climate, is readily acknowledged by the natives themselves, from whatever province of India they may have come. The monthly average of sick in hospital, as far as we could ascertain, appears to be 66, or 6 per cent. on the whole : we are unable to show in figures the gradual improvement which has taken place in the health of the men since their arrival, because hospital-books have not been generally kept, as is directed for the apprentices, in which the names of the sick, the dates of the doctor's visits, and the medical treatment prescribed, should be briefly entered; the adoption of such a measure, we think, would be advisable, and much facilitate the making periodical returns of the sick, on any future inquiry as to proper medical treatment being afforded them.

4. We have carefully inquired into the mortality that has taken place, both from the masters and the Indians. On a few of the estates it has been, we regret to say, considerable; but in no instance could it be attributed to over-work or ill-treatment. The two estates belonging to Messrs. Hanning and Harris, which we particularly noticed for that perfect harmony and contentment which follow good management and kind treatment of Indians, present the heaviest mortality. Mr. Harris had been but a short time on the estate, and could therefore afford no information as to the state of the men on their arrival. Mr. Hanning communicated to the committee a certificate, signed by a medical man, as to the state of the men he received; twelve were labouring under bad chronic diseases, five of whom subsequently died. No other planter has taken the same precaution as Mr. Hanning.

5. In asserting that the bodily health of the Indians in this district is improved, we are borne out by the figured statement of mortality, which, in four years, presents an average of 2·74 per cent.; and taking that of the two last years, which embraces a larger number of Indians, the result would be still more favourable, the average being reduced to 2·33 per cent.

6. We have not to bring to the notice of government any case of systematical bad treatment, or breach of contract on the part of the master; the men are treated with humanity and mildness, and the work required of them, although more severe than that to which they have been accustomed in India, is much within what they could perform in a climate like this, so much more favourable to bodily exertion than their own.

7. We would beg to suggest the necessity of some regulation calculated to remove a general tendency to misunderstanding between the master and labourer, arising out of the great discrepancies which exist in the conditions of the different contracts, principally with regard to food and the hours of labour; they are to be found even on the same estate, where bands of Indians have been introduced at different periods ; in some the articles of food are limited to rice and salt; an addition of a quarter of a rupee is sometimes made to the pay; but here it could never be considered as an equivalent for the ghee and dholl allowed them by other agreements.

8. In some of the contracts the Indian custom has been observed in fixing the hours of labour from sunrise to sunset, with an interval of three hours for meals; in others, they are from daylight till night; in others, again, they are left entirely to the discretion of the master, as will be seen by a reference to those abstracts of the different contracts we have annexed to our proceedings; where the hours are fixed, there is always a clause reserving to the master the right of extending the work, " if necessary," during the manufacturing season, that is, six months of the year.

9. We have communicated to the Indians the institution of a savings' bank in Port Louis, as affording a secure place of deposit for their money. We have met with about seventy men in this district who have saved money, one, a sirdar on Mr. Harris's estate, to the extent of six hundred rupees. It is to be observed, that more than half the number of the men we have examined have been but a short time in the island, and cannot yet have reimbursed the advances they are supposed to have received in India; the number of those that are provident would very rapidly increase, were the masters more generally to encourage habits of economy in the Indians.

10. We have found the Indians aware of the obligation of the master to provide a passage back after the expiration of the contract; but we noticed that a few of the planters have an idea, which we think erroneous, regarding the right of the Indian to stay in the island, otherwise than in the service of his first master. Several labourers have put the question to the members of the committee. Although we expressed an opinion in the affirmative as to their right, we would think it advisable that all doubts on the subject should be cleared up in their minds, as many, rather than stop with an unkind master at the expiration of their contract, might leave the island, under the erroneous impression of being unable to change for a better. It would be but just, however, that the masters should be relieved from all responsibility towards the government with regard to the Indian who leaves his service and remains in the island. This responsibility might be easily transferred to the Indian himself, by requiring the deposit in the savings' bank of the thirty rupees retained by the master to provide for a passage back, at the labourer's expense, in case of misconduct.

11. A few complaints of personal chastisement by overseers were made by labourers on some of the estates; we never found it to have been sanctioned or countenanced by the master : restraint has been employed only when necessary for the preservation of good order and discipline on the estate, such as in cases of drunkenness and riotous conduct. The power of punishing even the slave has for so many years been taken away from the master, and vested in a public officer, that we consider it improbable to suppose that a system of punishment by personal restraint and chastisement could be adopted towards free men, whom it is, moreover, so much the interest of the planter to conciliate in every way. On many estates the mere attempt at such a course of proceeding would have been attended with danger to the planter, for instead of the mild and inoffensive Hill Coolie, he would have had to deal with the bold and independent native of Western India, whose disposition would ill brook severity and harsh treatment.

12. We estimate, from the bands of Indians hitherto examined, that more than half of the men brought from the Bengal presidency are from the western provinces, where the duffadars and crimps found willing dupes to practise upon. The misrepresentation of the nature of the work, which many were led to expect would be mere (Baghee-chu-ka-kam) gardening, would not, from their distressed circumstances at the time (in consequence of the famine), have engendered a spirit of disappointment in those people on their arrival, had they not besides been plundered prior to embarkation of a great portion of the advances charged to the planters.

13. We will conclude with stating, that we are strongly impressed with the belief that the condition of the Indian in the island is superior to what it is in most parts of India; but the ideas of natives differ so widely from our own on those points, that the true test of their real sentiments can only be expected at the close of their engagements. We have seen in Port Louis several natives of Bombay, introduced by Mr. Bickerjee, who have entered into contracts with Mr. Des Etangs, at an increased rate of wages; it has also come to our knowledge, that several natives of the coast of Coromandel, lately in the employ of Mr. Darifat, in this district, having completed their five years' service, have formed a new engagement with Mr. Amadowmy, of the Riviere du Rampart district.

We have, &c.

(Signed)   C. M. CAMPBELL, President.

J. VILLIERS FORBES,
T. HUGON,   } Members.
J. BURY.

The Hon. Captain Dick, Colonial Secretary, Port Louis.

This letter brings to a close the labours of the Commissioners of Inquiry into the condition of the Coolies in Mauritius, and any thing more unsatisfactory can scarcely be imagined. If we may believe these gentlemen, the Coolies on the estates they visited are treated " with humanity and kindness;" but it is quite clear from the mi-

nutes of evidence, scanty as they are, as well as from the general
remarks in their own letter, that this statement must be received,
not only with great caution, but with great abatement. They call
attention to the " general tendency to misunderstanding between the
master and labourer, arising out of the great discrepancies which
exist in the condition of the different contracts, principally with regard to food and the hours of labour." Now, in no instance can it
be found that the quantity of rice given to the Coolie per week ex-
ceeds twelve pints, and in some] cases it is less, which is scarcely
more than *one-half* the quantity a labourer engaged in sugar cultivation requires to keep up his bodily strength ; as was sufficiently
proved in the case of the labourers in British Guiana. On one
estate, the " Laura," where the Coolies received the full quantity of
rice, the commissioners state that they " complain of not receiving a
sufficient quantity of rice." On " Marnet's Estate," they say, " Although they (the Coolies) receive the quantity of provisions accord-
ing to their engagement, yet they complain of its not being enough."
On plantation "Beauchamp, they complain of not receiving their
quantity of rice," though, the commissioners add, they " weighed the
ration, and found it correct." On Madame L'Emperna's estate,
though the Coolies got their one-and-a-half pounds of rice, salt,
" they say it is not enough." On Langlois' estate "they are dissatis-
fied with their engagement, as they receive but $1\frac{1}{2}$ lbs. rice, and $\frac{1}{4}$ oz.
salt." On Gelle's estate, "they are dissatisfied with the quantity
and quality of their provisions," though they get " $1\frac{1}{2}$ lbs. rice and
$\frac{1}{2}$ oz. salt." On several of the estates, " the Coolies complained of
not having sufficient time allowed them for repose and meals during
the day, being allowed from one hour and three quarters to two
hours only, instead of three hours ; and with respect to the amount
of work exacted, it appears they are generally required to labour
from sun-rise to sun-set, ordinarily, and during the season of crop for
such longer period of time as may be necessary : it appears also that,
on some estates, " they are obliged to fetch a bundle of grass each for
their employer, which occupies them till eight o'clock at night," or
to cut wood in addition to their daily toil. But the whole system
will be better understood by consulting the following "summary of
agreement with Indian labourers engaged by Mr. T. Francis for Mr.
Menage, and transferred to Mr. Blancard, of Beauchamp estate," and
which in reference to wages, food, and clothing, is more liberal than
most, if not all others, of which we have any account in these papers,
viz.—the Coolies are

1. Engaged to work for five years ; transfer to be made by mutual
consent before a public officer.

2. To perform all work on a sugar estate.

3. Hours of labour from sunrise to sunset, two hours allowed for
meals ; time of labour extended during the manufacturing of sugar,
if necessary.

4. To submit to such discipline as established by proprietor ; not
to absent themselves without written permission, under penalty of
half a rupee per diem, and any misunderstanding to be submitted to
a legal authority.

5. Medical aid to be borne by the master, except in cases of illness brought on by intemperance and misconduct. Labourers to receive no pay during illness.

6. One rupee to be retained from their wages to pay passage back, in case of misconduct.

7. The pay to commence from the date of their embarkation. Sirdars pay at seven rupees per month; five rupees to labourers; four rupees to first class boys, and three rupees to second class boys for the first two years, and four rupees for the remaining three.

Food,	14 chittacks of rice		1 ounce of ghee.
	2 do. dholl		$\frac{1}{2}$ ounce of salt.
Clothing, per annum,	2 dhooties		1 jacket.
	1 blanket		1 cap.

The whole system, as worked by a Mauritian planter, may be perfectly understood from this engagement, and we have no hesitation in saying it is one of gross imposition in its terms, and must be one of great oppression and suffering in its working. It should be observed, that, in cases of ill-treatment, the Coolies can only appeal for redress to the civil commissary of the Quarter or the Juge de Paix, both local officers, imbued with local prejudices, and often planters themselves.

On no estate does it appear that the commissioners inquired into the discipline practised on it; and, when instances of personal chastisement were brought to their notice, it was incidentally, and, as will be seen in their letter, treated lightly by them. On twelve estates out of the twenty-two, however, distinct cases of personal chastisement were brought under their attention, but no steps appear to have been recommended, or were taken, to punish the parties who were guilty of such illegal conduct. The opinion of the commissioners is worth nothing.

The few Coolies who have saved money are no doubt the "sirdars," or drivers of the gangs. It is their interest to make the people work, and in proportion to the zeal which they exhibit will be usually the reward they obtain.

Though no evidence appears on the minutes that the Coolies were brought to Mauritius otherwise than by their own consent, the commissioners nevertheless refer to the "duffadars and crimps" in India, who "found willing dupes to practise upon." What good results can be expected from a system engendered in fraud, and sustained by coercion? In an extract from the proceedings of the honourable the president in council in India, inserted in these papers, we find "that the methods adopted for procuring labourers to engage for service in colonies and places beyond sea are productive of serious frauds, and have led to much oppression, and that the system is a source of much injury and abuse, rather than of benefit to the labourers, in the form in which it is at present carried on." This extract is dated 11th July, 1838. The governor of Mauritius, at a subsequent period, adverting to the robbery and pillage of the Coolies previously to their leaving India, observes, that measures ought " to restrict the advance of wages" to them before their arrival in Mauritius, "so that," he adds, "the labourers, instead of finding themselves with several months' advance of wages to work out on their arrival here, may at once, or at least much earlier than at present, come into the receipt of wages for their labour, and *thus be enabled to provide themselves with such comforts as they may require, previously to their proceeding to the different estates on which they are to be employed."* How much of deplorable wretchedness and hardship does this sentence imply! Again, he observes, "The promised advance of wages, it is to be feared, is not faithfully accounted for to the emigrants; also that false descriptions have been given them, as well of the place they were going to, as of the nature of their employment there; and that there are instances in which Indians have been hurried on board ship, with whom no engagement had ever been made;" and, still further, he states, "In some cases, the proper allowance of food for the voyage has not been provided, medical inspection has not taken place previous to embarkation, nor medical attendance been furnished during the voyage!" Yet we are called upon to believe, in the face of all these facts, that the Coolies are so contented and happy, that they have no wish to change their situation! Finally, the commissioners, after having recorded in their minutes of evidence that the Coolies all "speak favourably of the island," and that they would "recommend their friends to come here," confess in their letter that they can scarcely credit them; for they say, "The ideas of natives differ so widely from our own on these points, that the *true test of their* REAL *sentiments can only be expected at the close of their engagements."* How valueless does this remark render the whole of the evidence of the Coolies, taken by these gentlemen in the presence of their masters, in which they are represented as saying that they are satisfied with their treatment! But, after all, it is apparent, that, in their estimation, slavery in Mauritius is only to be preferred to famine in India; so that it is quite clear, that the extreme wretchedness and poverty of the Coolie in his own country, arising from bad laws infamously administered, is the point of comparison in the judgment of the commissioners with what they found to be their condition in the colony, to which they had been brought by fraud or force, where, whatever might be their sufferings, they would not be exposed to the horrors of death by starvation.

No. II.

From the Anti-Slavery Reporter, May 6, 1840.

THE motion on which Lord John Russell has given notice, that he will take the opinion of the House of Commons, on the relaxation of the prohibition which at present exists, on the exportation of Coolies to Mauritius, stands for Friday, the 15th instant. It is, therefore, necessary that the friends of humanity should be on the alert, to prevent the scheme of the noble lord from being carried into effect. This may be done by numerous petitions against it, and by the different constituencies throughout the United Kingdom addressing respectful but decided letters to their representatives on the subject, and by earnestly entreating them to be in their places when the discussion shall come on, and to use their influence, and, if need be, their votes, to defeat the project.

The noble lord, in an admirable despatch to the governor of British Guiana, dated the 15th of February, 1840, referring to the further importation of Coolies into that colony, so ardently desired by the planters, says—" I confess I should be unwilling to adopt any measure to favour the transfer of labourers from British India to Guiana, *after the failure of the former experiment.* Admitting that the mortality of the Hill Coolies first sent may have been accidental, I am not prepared to encounter the responsibility of a measure which may lead to *a dreadful loss of life* on the one hand, or, on the other, to *a new system of slavery."*

The Guiana immigration ordinance, which provided for the further importation of Coolies, native Africans, and others, into the colony, was disallowed during the period Lord Normanby held the seals of the colonial office. The Trinidad ordinance also has been disallowed by the crown, in so far as it related to the import of labourers from Hindostan and Africa, since Lord John Russell has presided over that department; and it may be added, that both the noble secretaries have spoken in the most decided terms, in opposition to the earnest and oft-repeated solicitations of the planters of these colonies, to secure these classes of labourers. It may be asked, then, *why* the government intend to favour Mauritius? We are utterly at a loss to supply the answer. We know of no reason that can be given for it, which would not apply with greater force to Guiana and Trinidad, than to that colony.

It must be fresh in the recollection of the anti-slavery public of this country, that Mauritius was the *last* British colony to abandon the slave-trade, if indeed it were ever given up by that island; and the *last* to resist the wishes of the people and the government of this land, to terminate the apprenticeship system, the rigours of which in that colony were more terrible than those of slavery itself. One proof may be given: The quantity of food allowed the wretched apprentices was six pints of rye flour, or rice, or seven pounds of biscuit, or a proportionate quantity of vegetables, and three pounds and a half of salt-fish weekly, not *one-third* of the quantity secured to the slaves of the crown colonies by the order in council of 1832; and, to obtain the required amount of work from them, a most fearful amount of punishment was inflicted:—in twelve months, not less than 14,371 were punished, 7304 by the lash, on whom was inflicted the enormous amount of 135,124 lashes, and 7067 otherwise than by flogging, such as hard labour, penal gang in chains and collars, stocks, &c. &c. It will also be remembered, that the planters of this colony stand charged with the introduction of upwards of 30,000 slaves, after the slave-trade had been declared felony by the laws of England,

and that, notwithstanding the most palpable proofs of their guilt and criminality, they were not only permitted to escape the punishment which their atrocious offences merited, but, when the compensation money was distributed among the various colonies, their claims were admitted, and to the last farthing paid. It will be further remembered, that no colony has so insulted the mother country, violated her laws, and bid defiance to her power, as Mauritius; and what must appear passing strange, until the recent appointment of Sir Lionel Smith, scarcely a man, with the exception of General Hall, has swayed the government, who has not violated his trust, shrunk from the performance of his duties, or basely yielded to the French faction the executive power. One honest functionary after another has been displaced, the Jeremies have been thrust out to make way for the D'Epinays; and with scarcely a single exception, at the present moment, all the officers subordinate to the governor are the mere creatures of the pro-slavery party, which is made up, to use the language of Mr. Jeremie, "principally of the refuse of the French revolution," who entertain "a deadly hate of the principles, the manners, the power, the very name of Britain." The answer to the question proposed, *why* Mauritius is to be favoured, cannot be found in the humane character of its chief inhabitants, as planters, nor in their loyalty as subjects. On the blackest page in the annals of our colonies will be inscribed the history of Mauritius.

It is melancholy to reflect that previously to the prohibition on the export of Coolies having been issued by the governor-general of India, upwards of 40,000 had been introduced into that colony, under circumstances the most infamous, the larger part leaving behind them wives and children, parents and friends, to suffer the most cruel privations, or to perish with hunger in their native land. Those who went voluntarily were under the impression that they were going to the Company's "rabustie," or village, and that their employ would be "gardening," in return for which they were to have a sufficiency of food and clothing, besides the advantage of money wages. How were the miserable creatures deceived! They found that an island off the coast of Africa was their destination, and on their arrival there, that employments the most laborious were forced upon them, whilst their supplies of food and clothing were utterly insufficient for necessary purposes, and the money wages they were to receive were made to depend entirely upon the performance of the required amount of work. Any thing more heartless and cruel than the treatment of these people can scarcely be imagined. It is sufficient however to say that these things happened in Mauritius, to account for the villanies and deceits practised.

If the experience of the past should be any guide for the future, then we can perceive the strongest possible reasons why the government should stedfastly refuse the proposition of the Mauritians, made through their representatives and agents, Messrs. Irving and Barclay, in this country. These gentlemen have the strongest possible reasons for the exertions they have made, and are still making, to accomplish their purposes. In the *Cerneen*, a Mauritius paper, of the 21st of

December, 1839, the editor directed the attention of the public to the consideration of various schemes of immigration which were then current in the island, and after recommending the formation of a committee, who should " be charged with forming a project, and with afterwards transmitting it to our agents in London," adds, " But let it not have the power of doing any thing without the concurrence and approval of our London agents." " Who can tell," says the editor, " that the latter have not already acted in our behalf ? One of them has all his fortune at Mauritius, the others have twenty thousand tons of our sugar annually consigned to them." " Where," he asks in conclusion, " can men be found who are more vitally interested in the question?" In the succeeding paper the editor gives the news which had just reached the colony, "that Mr. Irving and Mr. Barclay had already taken active steps with Lord Normanby, as well as with his successor Lord John Russell, in order to procure the abrogation of the order in council prohibiting the emigration of Coolies, and the enactment of a new law respecting vagrancy." In a subsequent part of the communication, it is added: " Mr. Irving had framed a memorial, which he went, on the 14th of September, to present in person to Lord John Russell, at his private residence in Windsor Park. The interview, we are informed, was long, and Lord John Russell appeared to listen with considerable interest to the representations of Mr. Irving, who insisted principally, 1st. Upon the abrogation of the order in council prohibiting the emigration of Coolies; 2ndly. Upon the necessity of a new law respecting vagrancy ; and 3rdly. Upon the urgency of giving positive instructions to the stipendiary magistrates as to the line of conduct they are to pursue." Now, the whole of the proposition of Mr. Irving amounts to this— that the government should rescind the orders in council of the 7th of September, 1838, regulating contracts, and for the suppression of vagrancy, for the purpose of allowing the Mauritians to enter into contracts with the Coolies *in India* for a period of five years ; and when they get them there, to bring them under the operation of a stringent vagrant law, which should subject them to heavy punishments for "wandering abroad," or being found loitering on the public highways, or whistling in the streets of Port Louis ! And it would appear, that the special justices are to be instructed "as to the line of the conduct they are to pursue ;" in other words, they are to be coerced into subserviency to the will of the planters. We confess that we can scarcely trust ourselves to designate this monstrous proposition of Mr. Irving's, in language which shall at once indicate its true character, and his own daring ; but knowing, as we do, that the order in council regulating contracts is the only protection immigrants can have against the most shameful frauds, when application of its wholesome provisions is confided to the care of an upright stipendiary magistracy, and that the existing vagrant law is, in some of its enactments, even more stringent than it ought to be, we can conceive of nothing which deserves stronger censure, or more indignant reprobation, than this audacious attempt to revive the system and practice of slavery.

On one of the points so strenuously urged by Mr. Irving on the attention of Lord John Russell, we are happy to say the noble lord has given his positive assurance that no change shall take place : the order in council regulating contracts is to remain in full force, and of course the duties of the special justices under it will remain untouched. On another point, vagrancy, we trust the noble lord will be equally inflexible. The point gained by the Mauritians, is the relaxation of the prohibition on the export of Coolies from British India; but we feel persuaded that a determined resistance on the part of the country to this most unwise and impolitic measure will lead to its defeat.

It is difficult to fix the period when Coolies were first introduced into Mauritius. The references to the subject in the parliamentary papers we have been enabled to consult are exceedingly scanty. We find, however, in a despatch to Lord Glenelg, dated the 9th of September, 1837, Sir W. Nicolay states, " The number of Indians who have arrived here at different times within three years amounts to 8690, including women and children." From this extract it would appear, that the importation commenced before the termination of negro slavery in that colony. The terms on which they were engaged may be seen from the copy of agreement with thirty-six dhangars and Bhoond Coolies, by Arbuthnot and Co., Par. Pap. No. 74 (1838), from which we make the following extracts. "The pay of the natives shall be fixed at a rate of five rupees per month for each man," for "digging holes, weeding canes, or working in the sugar-house, *the quantity of daily labour required from each to be fixed by the manager of the property.*" Food allowed "for each man, per day, two pounds of rice, half-a-pound of dholl, and two ounces of salt, and some oil and tamarinds; and annually for each, four dhooties, one sheet, two blankets, one jacket, and two caps;" period of service, five years; and it was stipulated that one rupee per month should be deducted from their wages to form a fund, to provide them the means of return home after their contract was fulfilled. Subsequently to this period, we find the contracts less liberal, and the following may be quoted as the average of them, viz.: wages, three to five rupees per month, with one pound and a half of rice, four ounces of dholl, two to three ounces of salt fish, one ounce of ghee, half an ounce of salt per diem, with deductions in some cases of as much as two rupees per month, to repay advances for the expenses of voyage to Mauritius, and for the purpose of forming a fund to pay for the return of the Coolies to India at the expiration of their terms of service. In all cases further deductions were made for absent and sick days. The clothing annually supplied, " eight yards of common cloth or linen, two handkerchiefs, or two dhooties, one jacket, and one red cap." The usual time of labour, from sun-rise to sun-set, with two hours' relaxation for meals, except during crop-time, which lasts about six months in the year, when they are required to work as many hours as may be necessary.

The nature of the laws under which these Coolies were placed may be gathered from the remarks of Lord Glenelg, in a despatch to Sir William Nicolay, dated 25th May, 1836, conveying to him the disallowance of an ordinance, " to conciliate the maintenance of good order, and the demands of industry," &c. His lordship says, " The design of the law might more accurately have been described as *the substitution of some new coercion* for that state of slavery which has been abolished ; the effect of it, at least, is *to establish a compulsory system, scarcely less rigid, and in some material respects even less equitable, than that of slavery itself.*" Had his lordship used stronger language to designate this most iniquitous law, it would not have been inappropriate. For instance, labourers out of employ, or choosing to indulge themselves in temporary repose, might be adjudged to labour as convicts on the public works or on the plantations; and as Lord Glenelg states, " condemned without even the imputation of a fault to three years' compulsory labour ;" nay, his lordship goes further, and says that the operation of the law would be such as to inflict " compulsory labour for life on the labourers, on the plantations to which they may be assigned by the police."

The disallowance of this and another ordinance of a similar evil tendency " excited," as we are informed by Sir W. Nicolay, " a considerable degree of alarm ;" and he informs the government that petitions had been forwarded to him, soliciting permission to call a general meeting of the inhabitants for the purpose of drawing up a memorial "*protesting against the disallowance.*" Instead of indignantly refusing to receive the petitions, which were in their nature seditious, inasmuch as they dared to call in question the prerogative of the crown, the governor expressed himself in reply to them in the following terms : " Entertaining sentiments on the importance of that ordinance correspondent with your own, his excellency yet feels obliged to withhold his sanction from a meeting to be convened for the avowed purpose of protesting against an act of his majesty's, in the exercise of his royal prerogative." He then presumes to reason on the decision of his majesty as having caused him the greatest disappointment, and ventures indirectly to censure the course which the home government had felt it to be its duty to pursue ; he then adds, " Under the preremptory instructions to make immediate announcement of the disallowance, it became his excellency's duty to publish the fact, but his attention has ever since been occupied on this important subject, in the hope of devising some means for accomplishing the objects contemplated by the enactment of ordinance No. 16, without infringing upon the injunction conveyed by the secretary of state." Ought this man to have been allowed to hold office one moment after the government became aware of the course he had taken ? Yet he was permitted to retain it sufficiently long to give his sanction to several most infamous laws in defiance of the preremptory orders of the crown ; viz., a vagrant law (ord. No. 6, 1838) of the most oppressive character, which bears exclusively on the liberated negroes and the Coolies ; and in order to give full effect to it, another ordinance was passed, appointing a body of rural police (gardes champêtres) from which every proprietor may have two men on his estate on condition of paying a certain sum per month! These police are to be armed and equipped as the ordinary policemen, to live on the plantations of the proprietors, and, in point of fact, to form part of their establishments, and to be entirely under their direction and control. It is provided also, that these " gardes champêtres " shall, whenever required, be concentrated on any given spot. With such a body of men, paid, fed, and directed by the planters, it is easy to conceive that the liberties of the negroes and Indians in Mauritius are narrowed within the smallest possible compass. We have, in past numbers, adverted to the existence of this and other laws, which had been recently transmitted home, and trust that the government has sent out the notification of their disallowance to Mauritius by his excellency Sir Lionel Smith. The vagrant law was superseded by the order in council of the 7th Sept. 1838, but we have been assured, on authority direct from Mauritius, of a recent date, that the one referred to above is still administered as the vagrant law of the colony.

We have adverted to these points to show that hitherto not the slightest confidence could be placed in the good faith of the colonists, nor in the wisdom of the legislative council, nor in the firmness of the executive; and yet Mauritius is to have more Coolies!

We look almost in vain through the parliamentary papers for a straightforward and honest statement of the general treatment of the Indian labourers. On this important point, as well as on the state of the law, Lord Glenelg, in a despatch to Sir W. Nicolay, dated 14th May, 1838, thus writes:—" It appears *there is no law in force for regulating the duration of contracts of this nature,*" viz., *with the the Coolies, "for prescribing their terms, or for securing to the labourer, without the expensive and slow process of action at law, the faithful execution of these terms.*" " I also collect," adds his lordship, " that they are usually brought into the colony unaccompanied by females, thus aggravating the evils of the existing disproportion of the sexes ; and finally, that *it is apparent that your conclusions in favour of the present system rest upon the reports of the employers, and on those of the commissaries of quarters, who are, for the most part, if not wholly, engaged on their own account in the cultivation of land by the same or similar methods.*" In a subsequent despatch, dated 31st January, 1838, the noble lord calls the " special consideration" of Governor Nicolay to three points, " 1st, the absence of a proper proportion of women to accompany the Indians. 2dly, the want of an unexceptionable authority to settle disputes between the labourers and their employers. And, 3rdly, the limitation of the terms of the contracts." The mere statement of these points is sufficient to show the nature of the system under which the Coolies were brought, and the frauds and injuries to which they were exposed. References are occasionally made to Coolies who were imported into Mauritius, some as far back as 1830, without even the formality of a contract ; and it is not attempted to be denied that large numbers were so introduced. Mr. Scott, an eye-witness of the condition of many of them, pronounced it to be " deplorable ;" and says, that " some complained much of the *severity* and *duration* of their work ; that the *stipulated* quantity of food and clothes was not distributed ;" and " that the terms of these (contracts) are getting gradually *less advantageous to the Indian,*" as we have before shown, and that " *numbers were only restrained by being on an island from at once running away !*" We find also that " engagements had been entered into in Calcutta with the Indians," which required their " working on Sundays," which permitted their " corporal punishment by the sirdar, or chief," and which allowed the planters to exact from them " unlimited hours of work." Against irregularities of this kind the governor cautions the importers of these people into Mauritius ; but none of the evils complained of were remedied, up to the period when the governor-general of India issued a prohibition against their further exportation, either to that colony, or to the West Indies—a measure which the home government also, in consequence of the debates in both houses of parliament, and the disclosures then made, felt to be imperatively necessary to prevent the further traffic in the persons of the Coolies, which was declared to be second only in atrocity to the African slave-trade.

Mr. Scott, in his report to the governor-general of India, from which we have already quoted, states, that he found the Coolies in Mauritius had left India " under the impression that they were going to the company's rabustie," (or village,) and adds, " The only practical difference between the slaves and the Indians is that the latter receive remuneration in money." He afterwards observes, that the Indian infers from the statements made to him, " that the price of rice, ghee, &c. is the same at the rabustie, as ' in his own bazaar,' and only finds out his error when it is irretrievable."

Mr. J. P. Woodcock, of the Bombay civil service, made also a report to the governor-general of India on the same subject, from which we make a few short extracts. After stating the manner in which Coolies were obtained in Calcutta, through the medium of " crimps," he adds, " Mauritius was described to them in glowing terms, and advantage taken of their ignorance to provoke the belief that every necessary of life was cheap, labour light, and that the voyage would only occupy them ten days." Of their treatment on board ship during their voyage, he gives the following description :—" I was a passenger in March last in the *Drongan*, 355 tons, Captain Mackenzie, bound for Mauritius with a cargo of rice, and sixty-six Coolies, * * * * of every variety of caste from the Brahmin to the Choman. * * * * * The lower decks of the *Drongan* were stowed with rice, and the Coolies were disposed in the waist between the gangways and the forecastle, where, if the weather had not been remarkably fine, they might have suffered, *being unprotected from every change of weather.*"

He then informs us that " they were made to assist in working the ship, and suffered no ill-treatment but such punishment as their own sirdar inflicted." The voyage occupied two months in this instance. On their arrival, the Coolies " were marched off to their destination," to perform as much labour when there as " should be fixed by the manager of the estate," which he subsequently describes as "a long and hard day's work." He fully confirms Mr. Scott's representations respecting the price of "food and raiment in Mauritius," which, he remarks, "is inordinately expensive."

He found the Coolies were generally ignorant of the mode of obtaining redress for their grievances; and when not ignorant, they complained "of the distance to which they must proceed to obtain justice." On stating to them that they might apply to "the commissary of police of the division of the island to which their estate belongs," they replied, "He is a Frenchman, ignorant of our language; and then our master is a Frenchman; so what justice can we expect?" "The chief abuses," Mr. Woodcock adds, "which suggest themselves as possible to occur in the system at present adopted of procuring and deporting labourers to the Mauritius are, the manner in which they are collected; the ignorance of the terms on which they have agreed to serve; the doubt whether the identical persons who agree are embarked; and the treatment they are likely to obtain during the voyage."

The frightful mortality which has attended the transit of the Coolies to Mauritius must not be overlooked. Sir W. Nicolay, addressing the supreme government of India, points out "the necessity of measures for the proper treatment of the Coolies on the passage," and subsequently goes on to state, "that three successive ships have been placed in quarantine, owing to *the disease and extensive mortality* that has prevailed among the labourers embarked upon them;" that the *William Wilson*, out of 224, had lost 31; the *Indian Oak*, 6; and the *Adelaide*, out of 72, no fewer than *twenty-four*, besides *two* on its arrival, and *one* lost overboard. And the colonial secretary (Dick,) in a despatch to the government of Madras, attests that "the ship *Edward Robinson*, of 300 tons burthen, brought from Pondicherry and Tranquebar 425 natives of India," and adds, "*On board which ship there was no surgeon*, nor any person capable of giving professional assistance, in case of sickness or an accident occurring." "In the instance of the *Juliana*," says Sir. W. Nicolay, again, "very unfavourable rumours reached the government, after her departure, of *the manner in which the Indians on board of her were treated*, the truth of which I have reason *not* to doubt." One extract more from the parliamentary papers before we quit them; "I have heard a case," says Mr. Scott in his paper laid before the governor-general of India, "where the old slaves of an estate had come to their master, and begged him to send for no more Indians to take the bread out of their mouths." In how many cases this may have been done we know not; but we can easily imagine what must have been the effect of the introduction of about 40,000 Coolies, all of whom, with the exception of a few hundred women and children, were *adult* labourers, upon the interests, and the happiness, as well as the morals of the liberated negroes; and we do know, that the great object for which this host of Indians has been imported into Mauritius has been to lower the price of wages, by compelling the negroes to accept such terms as their masters choose to give them, or to starve!

In answer to the question, " How were the Coolies in Mauritius obtained previously to the restrictions being laid on?" Mr. Prinsep, secretary to the government of India, in an official report on the subject, states : "The methods adopted for procuring labourers to engage for service in colonies and places beyond sea, are productive of serious frauds, and have led to much oppression, and," he further observes, " the system is a source of injury and abuse rather than of benefit to the labourers, in the form in which it is at present carried on." To go into the history of all those "frauds" would be to detail circumstances second only in atrocity to those connected with the African slave-trade. The fact is established beyond dispute, that multitudes have been kidnapped—forced into prison-depôts until the Mauritian slavers were ready to receive them—hurried on board— put under hatches and guards—robbed and pillaged of the advances made to them by the Mauritian agents in Calcutta—shipped in large numbers on board vessels without the requisite accommodation, food, or medical attendance—brought under the most fraudulent contracts to labour for years on scanty wages, and scanty fare—separated from their families and from their homes—compelled to perform the hardest agricultural labour known at the discretion of their masters— and, to crown all, left without the protection of an upright, impartial, and efficient magistracy.

As to the general treatment of the Coolies in Mauritius, but one opinion can be entertained by the friends of humanity. Independently of the evidence derived from private sources, on which implicit reliance can be placed, which represents the state of the Coolies as deplorably wretched, and their hardships and sufferings as even greater than those endured by the negroes when slaves, the fact of their having become the prey of the Mauritian planters, would be sufficient to justify the worst apprehensions that could be entertained on that point. One honest functionary in Mauritius, Mr. Special Justice Anderson, has spoken out upon this point, in opposition to those who would have us believe that the Coolies in that colony are treated with " humanity and kindness ;" and, we have no doubt, in opposition to his own interests and personal ease and comfort. In his letters to Governor Nicolay, dated the 19th and 30th of November, 1839, he states, that those whom he had examined in Port Louis were " overworked," were subjected to severe " personal chastisement," were without proper shelter and " lodging accommodation," were deprived of necessary medical attendance and care when suffering from disease, and in other ways seriously injured and abused, insomuch that he says, " It is a source of astonishment to me that any body of freemen, whatever may have been their former condition, should have borne, with the patience and forbearance which the Indian labourers at Port Louis have displayed, *the bitter disappointment which must have attended their introduction into this island;*" and, he adds, " To induce them to come here, their ignorance is worked upon in India by the most false and deceitful representations, and the robbery and pillage which has been practised on them at Calcutta would scarcely be credited, if the fact was not established by the most convincing testimony. They reach this colony after having been robbed of six months pay, which is advanced (or said to be advanced) in India; and when here their comfort is in every way neglected, while they are compelled by the engagements to which their own ignorance or the avarice of others has bound them, to toil during five years for a recompence bearing no proportion to the work to which they are subjected, when compared with the common estimation of the value of labour in this colony, or to the sum which they would earn if they had the free disposal of their own time."

But it may be said, that the evils we have glanced at are admitted, and that the object of the government is to prevent their occurrence in future. Lord John Russell would extend the clauses of the colonial passengers' act to Mauritius, to prevent the overcrowding of vessels carrying emigrants from Hindostan to that colony, and for securing to them a sufficient supply of food and water, and of medical treatment and care while on board. We can have no possible objection to this, but we would remind the noble lord that all this was said to have been provided for long ago by the governor-general of India, and that, notwithstanding the existence of the regulations, and the vigilance of the public officers in the different presidencies, the evils complained of multiplied and increased to so serious an extent as to compel the supreme government to interdict the further progress of emigration. We observe also that the laws in force affecting the labourers in Mauritius require a most careful examination and revision, before the government would be justified in taking off the interdict. We affirm, without fear of contradiction, that the whole correspondence between the executive of that island and the colonial office, if it were made public, would show, that up to the present period, the laws which have been enacted and are in force are of the most atrocious nature, with the exception only of those orders in council issued in 1838, which we have the most serious grounds for believing are a dead letter. We affirm also, that if all the papers and documents now in the colonial office respecting the Coolies were published, the noble lord would scarcely venture upon the step he proposes to take on the 15th inst. At all events, we ask whether the reports of the commissioners of inquiry in India which led Lord Auckland to interpose the supreme authority of India, for the protection of the Coolies, ought not to be produced before any measures be adopted which shall relax the restrictions which at present exist to their further exportation; and is it not reasonable to expect that the present governor, Sir Lionel Smith, should be called upon to report on the actual condition of those already in Mauritius; the state of the law which affects them; and the measures which may be necessary to secure them ample protection, before the Mauritian planters be permitted to reduce any more to what we believe will be found, on inquiry, a system of slavery? We implore the noble lord to defer his proposition until the British public and the British parliament are in a position to decide upon these important measures.

It cannot be argued that there has been so diminished a supply of the staple products of Mauritius raised since the emancipation of the slaves took place, as to render such a measure as that contemplated by the noble lord necessary. In 1825, the quantity of sugar exported was 93,723 cwts.; in 1829, 297,958 cwts.; in 1833, 529,352 cwts.; in 1837, 537,961 cwts.; in 1838, 604,671 cwts.; and in 1839, 612,385 cwts. Here, then, we have full proof that the arguments so incessantly urged by the West India colonies, and which have been so well met by the noble lord at the head of the colonial department, in a recent despatch to the governor of British Guiana, will not apply to Mauritius.

We ask for time and for further information, which we know the government possess or ought to possess; and earnestly trust the noble lord who proposes to open India once more to the planters of Mauritius will re-consider the subject, and postpone the contemplated measure, at least until another session of parliament. But should the noble lord persist in urging it forward, we entreat those honourable members who have distinguished themselves, without reference to party, as the enemies of oppression, and the friends of liberty, to give it their strenuous and most decided opposition.

In conclusion, we call the attention of our readers to a circular addressed to each member of parliament on the 26th of March last, when the discussion was expected to come on, by the committee of the British and Foreign Anti-Slavery Society, and which we need not say is as applicable now as it was then:—

The Committee of the British and Foreign Anti-Slavery Society deeply regret to find, contrary to their earnest hope, that the government have determined, in connexion with the extension of the "Colonial Passengers' Bill to Mauritius," by the clauses to be proposed by Lord John Russell, to seek the sanction of the House of Commons to the relaxation of the prohibition which at present exists against the exportation of Coolies from Hindostan.

The committee respectfully but earnestly implore your attendance at the House to-morrow, Friday evening, to prevent the adoption, or, at least, to postpone the consideration of so injurious a measure until some future session of the House, for the following among other reasons:—

1. Because an immense number of Coolies, amounting to more than 40,000, have already been introduced into that colony under circumstances the most infamous, and held to service under contracts the most fraudulent; leaving in India, as is well known, in the great majority of instances, their wives and children, destitute and without protection.

2. Because the official accounts which have been received in reference to them state the startling fact, that out of upwards of 19,000 Coolies (the number reported), scarcely more than 200 were females.

3. Because the very partial inquiry into the condition of the Coolies in Mauritius, conducted under circumstances in no wise likely to elicit truth, and extending to not more than 2,500 of them, is of the most meagre, unsatisfactory, and contradictory character.

4. Because the governor-general of India, in consequence of the

c 2

atrocities brought to light by a court of inquiry held on the spot, in connexion with the mode in which they had been obtained and transported to Mauritius, absolutely forbad their further exportation to that or any other British colony, from any of the presidencies.

5. Because neither the report of the commissioners of inquiry in India, which led the governor-general to take this most decided and important step, nor the communications of that high functionary to the home government stating his reasons for the same, nor the despatches of her Majesty's ministers relative thereto, have been presented to parliament.

6. Because the home government fully confirmed, in the year 1838, the previous decision of the governor-general of India, after a full discussion of the whole question in both houses of parliament.

7. Because the state of the law in Mauritius, at the present time, as affecting every class of labourers, is of the most rigorous and oppressive kind, and is chiefly administered by the planters themselves.

8. Because the demand for an augmentation of labourers is principally grounded on an alleged want of disposition to industry, and a reasonable demand for wages on the part of the negro freemen, of which no proof appears, and which is contrary to the general evidence furnished in those instances, in any of the colonies in which they have been considerately and equitably treated.

9. Because the amount of produce raised in Mauritius, so far from showing a diminution since the abolition of slavery, exhibits an immense increase.

10. Because, from the facts already established in the papers laid before parliament, the most rigid and searching inquiry, conducted by impartial, disinterested, and honourable men, is imperatively demanded, before the government can be justified in taking so important a measure as that about to be submitted for the sanction of parliament.

PARLIAMENTARY PROCEEDINGS.

HILL COOLIES.

On Thursday, June 4th, 1840, Lord John Russell brought forward his long pending motion for removing the restrictions imposed upon the transportation of the Hill Coolies of our eastern possessions to Mauritius.

His lordship, in moving his clauses, said, that those clauses were intended to bring before the house the general question, as to whether, under any restrictions which might be devised, the prohibition now existing might be removed, in reference to the exportation or removal of Hill Coolies from India to Mauritius. He thought that the prohibition which had been imposed last year (looking at all the horrors which had accompanied the importation of Coolies) was the best measure which could have been resorted to, to remove the evil, until further legislation should take place. But some time had now elapsed, and the question had caused much discussion, and he thought that the house would now be enabled to frame sufficiently stringent restrictions to prevent those gross abuses which had formerly been found to prevail. He thought it would be necessary, in the first place, to take care that the agents to be appointed in India, should be so appointed by the governor-general of India, or by some other person holding superior authority in India, who (from their position) would not allow any of those abuses which had been complained of to take place again. In the next place, he held it to be absolutely necessary to maintain the principle of the order in council with respect to the colonies, namely—that when those persons arrived in the Mauritius they should be free to make such contracts as they should think fit for their own benefit, for periods of one year and no longer. He thought that there should be certain provisions made for the introduction of females as well as for the men, *with a view to prevent the recurrence of those frightful scenes which had occurred*, but which, he hoped, would not again take place in any future emigration. With restrictions of this kind, backed as they would be by orders in council, by instructions to the governor of Mauritius, by instructions from the Board of Control, and to the governor-general of India, he thought this emigration might be allowed. The clauses were very general, but he thought that the papers which were on the table were sufficient to show that when these restrictions were placed in the hands of those who would be appointed by the English authorities, they would be duly carried into effect. He thought that they might safely rely upon the conduct of those persons in whom it was intended to place the power of appointment. He thought there was a great difference between allowing Hindoos from India to emigrate to the Mauritius and allowing them to migrate to the West Indies, because there would always be a strong objection to introducing into the West Indies a new race, a third race of men—amongst the natives of the soil, men of totally distinct habits. And they were to consider the comparative distance of India from the West Indies as compared to the Mauritius, and the difficulty, in the former case, of the Coolies being returned to their own country. He thought that these were sufficiently strong reasons for the prohibition of the importation of Coolies into our West Indian possessions. He must add that the papers which had last been presented to the house, were sent home by the governor of the Mauritius, with his strong recommendation; and that a committee of gentlemen, proprietors of estates in the Mauritius, had chosen Mr. Anderson, a gentleman who was well known, to bring their case before the government.

Sir EARDLEY WILMOT, Mr. BERNAL, Mr. HOBHOUSE, Mr. C. BULLER, and other hon. members took part in the debate. We have room, however, for only the material parts of it.

Dr. LUSHINGTON deeply regretted the question had come in such a form before the house. It had been charged against the opponents of the introduction of Hill Coolies as labourers, that they were opposed to the introduction of all free labour into the colonies. That was not true, for one of the principles the opponents advocated was, that when there existed a want of labourers on one hand, and a superfluity of labourers on the other, the deficiency ought to be supplied on terms of mutual benefit. Again, it had been said the opponents were inimical to the sugar market; that they also disregarded the numerous petitions on the subject, and the high price of sugar which the consuming population were likely to be obliged to encounter. It was singular, however, that this outcry had arisen so soon. This deficiency had not yet become so alarming. There was as yet only a deficiency of one-tenth compared with last year, and thus there appeared no real grounds for assuming that the deficiency would be so great as to create inconvenience to the community. In answer to the remark that the deficiency of labour would create a still larger deficiency of produce, he had only to observe that all rational men must be agreed in the opinion, that it was a wise course to increase, as much as possible, the produce of sugar by the help of free labour. But the difficulty he had on the subject was from other and different considerations. As to the clauses, they were ostensibly to enable government to carry into effect the importation of Hill Coolies into the Mauritius. So far so good. But what he wanted to know was this—government had already made the experiment, the Indian government had tried all that lay in their power to prevent abuses, and government had been repeatedly told that the authority exerted to the utmost extent had utterly failed to repress abuses— (hear). From day to day, and hour to hour, men were kidnapped and sent away from India; he had the fact from a report, and from papers which he held, and this in addition, that 250 had been sent away in a single ship, in spite of the opposition of the authorities— (hear, hear). He asked his right honourable friend if he was going to arm government with greater powers if he succeeded in carrying his resolution. There was a report, but government had never produced it.

Sir J. C. Hobhouse—The report never arrived.

Dr. Lushington—That was very extraordinary, for he found the report in the very paper he held.

Sir J. C. Hobhouse said there was another report.

Dr. Lushington—It had been asserted that he was arguing on a report never made nor sent, but that a report was made he ascertained from the paper. The committee appointed to search into the subject had made a report, but that report had not as yet been produced. Now it was an important point to have this report. He wanted the report, because it would enable him to see if the exportation which had taken place was either deceptious or oppressive. The house ought to be satisfied on that head before it proceeded further with the affair. The report on the subject, which had obtained publicity, was from a gentleman, who declared that the frauds which had been committed were beyond conception, and utterly beyond the power of the government to prevent. The noble lord might state, in defence of his plan for exporting labourers from the East Indies, that he would bring forward an effectual and perfect remedy against those frauds and that injustice which had hitherto taken place ; but even if the noble lord did so, what was to become of the exportation from territories which did not belong to the British crown ?

Sir J. Hobhouse—There is no prohibition now.

Dr. Lushington—What he intended to convey was, that there was no safeguard of any kind against fraud and injustice. He would now advert to the middle passage. What were the regulations ? At present they were as stringent as possible, but yet they were baffled, and they afforded no real protection against wrong. He referred to past experience, and he wished to know what was the security the noble lord could offer for the enforcement of any one order in council he might obtain. He would defy contradiction of these facts. In 1810 we had the colony. In 1814 it was made a capital felony to import slaves. The report stated that out of the 30,000 slaves, 25,000 felonies had occurred. Subsequent to this, there was a registration, and it turned out the law had been so disregarded that of the total number of slaves, 30,000, there were 20,000 cases of fraud. In all the departments there existed fraud, and, with the exception of one officer, Sir Lionel Smith, no reliance was to be placed on any functionary. Justice was poisoned in the Mauritius from the top to the bottom. He (Dr. Lushington) presented a petition from some merchants, who declared they could not any longer carry on business if a better system of justice was not adopted in the Mauritius. What arose from this ? Why, that make what ordinance the house pleased, in the present state of things in the Mauritius, it would become a mere dead letter, and would never be carried into effect—(hear). In page 36 of the letters relating to the Hill Coolies, it was asserted that the labourers were overworked, and were subjected to personal chastisement—(hear). In case of sickness culpable neglect was exercised. From what he had remarked, he hoped it would not be inferred that he was opposed to voluntary emigration. On the contrary, if an effectual system was brought forward, so as to prevent those evils which existed, he was entirely in favour of the principle. But look how emancipation worked in the West Indies. The so-called free labourers worked under the notice of a police inspector. Those manumitted men were slaves to all intents and purposes—(hear). They could not leave their work or estate for even a short period without a ticket of leave—(hear). This was a mockery of freedom. And, though the munificent grant of £20,000,000 was destined to liberate the slaves, it was nothing less than a mockery and a fallacy to call them free labourers—(hear). He called attention to the mortality, which amounted to 8 or 9 per cent. yearly ; this alone ought to serve to show that the present system was the worst which could be adopted. The practice which had prevailed tended to degrade human nature, and to destroy human peace and prosperity. Although, in a vast number of cases, it was clearly proved that contracts had been violated, yet not one instance could be brought forward of justice having been done. In the Mauritius there were 30,000 males imported into a population of 60,000—(hear). It had been asserted that the planters were in distress, and that they were decreasing their growth of sugar. Precisely the reverse was the case. In 1823 the produce was 93,000 hogsheads, and this year it was 612,000—(hear, hear). From this, he argued, there was no immediate necessity for the present measure, and that, in fact, it could not be carried into operation with justice to the other colonies—(hear). He wanted, however, to know what consequences were to follow, were the same evils as heretofore to exist? He wished to see the whole subject before the house. He wanted the regulations to be well considered by the house, and to be established by the house. He wanted the executive principle to be so applied as not to be a dead letter, but to be carried into execution in every quarter of the globe. He had no hesitation in declaring his firm belief that the present diminution of the sugar produce would be less from time to time. He wished to extend the comfort of sugar to all classes, provided, in so doing, the principle of slavery was not fostered, under pretence of encouraging the system of free labour. With the exception of the governor going out, he knew of no individual connected with the Mauritius, in whom confidence could be placed. If additional powers were not conferred, the noble lord might make an order in council, but it would not be executed. If a better system were contained in the clauses than the one which now prevailed, he would have given them his support; but, as in his judgment this was not the case, he must withhold his support from them.

On the division the numbers appeared,

For the motion.............................79
Against it..................................44
Majority..................... —35

No. III.

From the Anti-Slavery Reporter, March 24, 1841.

It will be recollected that, in the parliamentary proceedings of last year, frequent reference was made to an official inquiry instituted by the government of India respecting the exportation of Coolies, and a consequent report, not then received in this country, but indispensable to any satisfactory proceeding. This document, so highly important and so loudly called for, has at length arrived, and has been printed by order of the House of Commons.

It appears that on the 1st of August, 1838, the secretary to government wrote to T. Dickens, Esq., the Rev. H. J. Charles, W. Dowson, Esq., Major Archer., Russomoy Dutt, Esq., and J. D. Grant, Esq., C. S., informing them that the deputy governor had selected them as a committee, to investigate the alleged abuses of the system of Coolie exportation. The committee commenced their operations on the 22nd of August, between which period and the 14th of January, 1839, they held not less than fifty sittings, and examined between thirty and forty witnesses, besides carrying on a considerable correspondence. The report is signed by only three of the gentlemen, who constituted the committee; Major Archer having left Calcutta pending the inquiry, and Messrs. Grant and Dowson differing in opinion on some points. We extract the following passages:—

"9. We conceive it to be distinctly proved beyond dispute, that the Coolies and other natives exported to Mauritius and elsewhere were (generally speaking) induced to come to Calcutta by misrepresentation and deceit, practised upon them by native crimps styled duffadars and arkotties, employed by Europeans and Anglo-Indian undertakers and shippers, who were mostly cognizant of these frauds, and who received a very considerable sum per head for each Coolie exported.

"10. That, if the natives in the interior, Hill Coolies or others, had been distinctly made aware that they were to go beyond seas to a great distance, and to remain absent for five years, it is probable that not one, or at least that very few, would have been induced to take such an engagement.

"11. That the Coolies seem generally to have been induced, by the duffadars and others employed in that business, to come to Calcutta, by being persuaded that they should find employment as peons under the company, work on the public roads, or as gardeners, porters, &c.

"12. That, in the case of the Hill Coolies especially, and in many other instances, the parties were really incapable of understanding the nature of the contracts they were said to have entered into, even when an opportunity of explanation had been afforded apparently sufficient for the purpose.

"13. That, in despite of the regulations of 1837, and the interference of the police, an impression was successfully created and maintained up to the date of the suspension of the trade, among the Coolies, that they would be liable to penal consequences if they expressed dissatisfaction at being sent on board ship; and this seems to have induced them, both previous to their departure and their return, to suppress the mention of their grievances wherever they conceived themselves interrogated by government officers.

"14. That kidnapping prevailed to a very considerable extent; and that the Coolies, while kept in Calcutta itself and its neighbourhood, were actually in a state of close imprisonment.

"15. That, notwithstanding the existence of these practices of kidnapping and illegal imprisonment, to a very great extent within the local limits of Calcutta itself, the police authorities of the town do not seem to have been well-informed of the facts; and it is certain that, whatever measures were adopted, such measures were completely ineffectual as a check upon these abuses.

"16. That the advance, as it was called, of six months' wages, seems to have been real as far as the planter wishing to import Coolies was concerned, and nominal as far as the Coolie was concerned. The planter paid the whole money, yet the Coolie received but little or nothing, until Sergeant McCann's interference. His mode of adjusting the accounts between the Coolie and the agent, or person that shipped the Coolies, was, in all cases, to allow the latter to retain twenty rupees of the money of each Coolie, out of which the trifling articles of clothing and utensils furnished to him were paid; the charges of Mr. Hughes, and other intermediate and subordinate crimps, such as the duffadars and arkotties; and lastly, the charge of Sergeant McCann himself. This system of nominal allowances to the Coolie was a source of fraudulent and dishonest gain to all the subordinate agents engaged in the export; and it is certain that, if advances were forbidden, the prop and mainstay of the Coolie trade, as heretofore carried on, would be at once removed. It will be observed, that, of the different parties engaged in the procuring and shipment of Coolies, not one tendered the production of his accounts.

17. That the legislative enactments and regulations of police made and passed for the prevention of abuses and due regulation of the trade in Calcutta, were of very little effect when enforced at all ; for, though it appears that some amelioration was affected after the Act of 1837, yet the foregoing well-established facts abundantly bear out the general conclusion. We may further remark, that it has been proved by the evidence of Captain Rapson, that, out of 336 Coolies which he carried to Mauritius in the *Sophia* in October 1836, only 140 were embarked while the ship he commanded was at her moorings, and the rest (that is to say, very nearly two-thirds) during her progress down the river, and without any pass or permit from the police at all. The only inference to be drawn is, that the laws and regulations of Calcutta restrictive of the illegal export of Coolies, can be evaded to any extent the shipper and captain may choose, and this with the utmost ease and impunity.

18. It may be further inferred that the laws and police regulations of Mauritius were not of much greater practical utility in restraining the illegal importation of Coolies, because, if strictly observed, the greater number of the Coolies carried by Captain Rapson in the *Sophia* must have been sent back, as shipped against the restrictive laws and regulations of Calcutta, of which the Mauritius police authorities were, as already observed, previously made aware ; but it appears from Captain Rapson's deposition, that they were all received and divided equally among the planters.

19. It further appears, from the evidence of the native witnesses taken as a whole, and after all due allowance made for a habit of exaggeration prevalent among Bengalees and Hindostanees, that the local police of the interior of Mauritius was not very accessible to complaints; that the regulations of the plantations are such as closely to resemble imprisonment within their boundaries, and that the magistrates of the interior are not very cordially disposed to enforce those provisions of the contract inserted for the advantage of the Coolie.

"20. It further appears (although the despatches of the Mauritius to the Bengal government would seem to make it doubtful whether these persons were imported in French vessels)to be distinctly proved by Mr. Dowson's evidence, that, since this export trade in Coolies from India to Mauritius began, more Coolies were exported from Pondicherry than from Calcutta and other Indo-British ports, or at least as many, and great numbers from Madras to a French colony in which slavery prevails. It follows that all precautionary and restrictive measures adopted merely in British ports are but of comparatively small utility, and will, if they should prove effective in any degree, end in driving the trade to foreign ports, if Mauritius or the West Indies are permitted to receive Coolies from them, as well as from our own.

"21. The hardships and miseries endured by the Coolies in the passage to Mauritius are proved to have been very great, under the most favourable circumstances, and with the most humane commanders, acquainted with the language and manners of the natives, the mortality from drowning and other causes was most serious. We are fully persuaded, that, if the emigration to Demerara and the West Indies were permitted, the mortality in the voyages, taken together, would not fall much short of 10 per cent. on the numbers exported.

"22. It appears in evidence that no restraint has at any time existed on the emigration of women, yet very few have gone. The Mauritius government has really been desirous that they should be sent; but we think it may be fairly inferred that the planters have not. The result of the emigration that has already taken place has been most disastrous to the families of those who have emigrated; and it is shown by the memorandum furnished to the Landholders' Society by Mr. Taylor, that the districts of Bancoorah and Maunbhoom have been burdened with a vagrant and mendicant population of paupers, composed of the deserted families of emigrant Coolies.

"23. On the subject of the condition of the Coolies in Mauritius, there is contradictory evidence. Mr. Onslow, of the Madras Civil Service, the Rev. Mr. Garstin, Dr. Wise, Captains Mackenzie and Rayne, (all unexceptionable witnesses in point of good faith, character, and veracity,) bear testimony to their healthy appearance and their apparent contentment, and seem to consider them as improved in condition. The natives, however, who have returned, with the exception of one Ramdeen, gave evidence the other way. It must be admitted, on such questions, these persons, however ignorant, are really the best judges. The European gentlemen would, from their own position in society, and their natural dispositions, associate probably only with planters of the superior classes and of humane tempers, whose treatment of their Coolie labourers would, it may be reasonably presumed, be liberal and considerate. And when an opinion is pronounced that the condition of a Coolie is bettered at Mauritius, it should be first ascertained what that condition was in India, and what is the condition of his wife and children, or those of his family dependent upon him, when left behind. Any benefit derived from the superiority of climate at Mauritius or elsewhere may, we think, very reasonably be put out of question, as a mere European notion. It is clear, however, that, if the contracts be fulfilled with perfect good faith, the individual Coolie temporarily betters his condition by emigrating to Mauritius, because he gets higher money wages, and food and clothing found him beside, though he has to work harder than in India. But it is clear also from the evidence, that the contracts, generally speaking, are not fulfilled by the planters. The conclusion of our minds from the whole evidence is, that these contracts have been strictly and literally fulfilled in no instance. Under good masters, there may be substantial fulfilment in good faith, as far as the circumstances of the island, in respect of imports of the kind of food stipulated for, permit, an equivalent being provided when the thing stipulated for cannot be afforded. In the majority of cases, however, there is nothing like that kind of performance shown; but, on the contrary, rice, salt, and clothing seem to be all that the Coolies do actually receive from bad masters; and no money wages at all seem to be paid in the majority of instances."

The committee subsequently advert to the question of resuming the "trade" in Coolies, on which they express themselves in the following decided terms:

" 27. We are thoroughly and intimately persuaded from our knowledge of this country, of the working of judicial and police establishments in the interior and in Calcutta itself, of the character of the natives, and of those classes of persons who would engage actively in promoting the export of Coolies here, and whom government would be compelled to employ in the practical supervision of of the details of all regulations to prevent abuse, whether in the interior or in Calcutta, that scarcely any human precaution would avail to prevent a repetition of abuses. However, abuses quite as gross as those which have already prevailed, in despite of the acts and regulations already passed, might perhaps be rendered rare. But no system, we are firmly convinced, would ever suffice completely to counteract the tricks and falsehoods that would be resorted to in India by the duffadars, arkotties, and other persons engaged in similar avocations.

" 28. We are also convinced that no regulations, nor even any such as we have subsequently pointed out as absolutely necessary, would after all, in practice, suffice to secure the emigration or export of a due proportion of women, or emigration by families. The interests of all classes of private persons concerned as exporters or importers are against it, and they will always operate more successfully than any laws or regulations that can be devised. Besides, it appears to be contrary to the general Asiatic character, and opposed to the feelings and prejudices of even the lowest classes, to emigrate with their women or families. There are thousands of Chinese emigrants at Singapore, and hundreds of thousands, we might even estimate by millions, in Siam, Java, Borneo, Manilla, and the islands of the Eastern Archipelago; of women there are few or none. Certainly the laws of China do, as it is said, prohibit the emigration of women; but as they equally prohibit the emigration of men, the true reason of the rarity of female emigrants must be sought for elsewhere; and it will be found in the jealousy and prejudices of Asiatics with regard to the female sex, in the want of due accommodation for women in maritime emigration, and in the extreme poverty of the emigrants, which leads them to abandon all family ties as an encumbrance, which, unable to bear at home, they are doubly unwilling to sustain abroad.

" 29. We doubt, moreover, whether any regulations in the island of Mauritius will suffice to secure the strict and just performance of any contracts. Of the state of things in the West Indies we are uninformed by evidence. Further, we think, that no contracts really as just and beneficial to the Coolie as they ought to be would be entered into, if the regulations were so enforced as that a near approach were made towards a strict enforcement of performance.

" 30. We are convinced, in fine, that no laws or regulations likely to be passed, short of making the whole land and sea transport of Coolies government services, superintended by government officers and medical men, will suffice to prevent great misery and distress, even on this side of the Cape; and that, if West Indian voyages be permitted, the waste of human life and misery that will fall on the Coolies exported under the name of free labourers, will approach to those inflicted on the negro in the middle passage by the slave-trade. The numbers of Coolies exported to Demerara, Berbice, and Essequibo, to Trinidad, Jamaica, and the West India islands generally, would probably be very great; the cost of the voyage there and back would be very heavy, particularly if short terms of contract were enforced and the impossibility of preventing exportation (whether professedly regulated or merely illicit) from foreign European ports and native territories in India complete. We think the latter consideration quite decisive against the expediency of re-opening the trade, when we reflect that, in addition to Danish, there are Portuguese and French ports and territories, from which a very large exportation could easily be organized. A prohibition to receive Coolies into British colonies in foreign vessels, might no doubt be enforced, but the exportation to foreign colonies could not be checked, except by long negotiations, if it were once begun, and our government would have no reason to urge for remonstrance or interference, that could not be answered by a reference to its own example, and on the general and abstract principles, that it is always an advantage to all countries where labour is dear, to import it from those where labour is cheap; and that it is the right of all men to trade in free labour, and especially of him whose only property is his capacity to labour, to sell that commodity to the best profit.

" 31. It seems to us that the permission to renew this traffic would weaken the moral influence of the British government throughout the world, and deaden or utterly destroy the effect of all future remonstrances and negotiations respecting the slave-trade, and this effect would ensue, however stringent, minute, or restrictive might be the regulations framed to check abuses. Regulations would be met by other regulations, specious and unobjectionable in form; the difference would be in the execution and in the good faith of the framers.

" 32. Moreover, we think, as far as India is concerned, the supreme government and the government of each presidency would be harassed by the occurrence of political disputes with the governments of foreign possessions, in addition to the labours of the watchful superintendence which would be required to be exercised, even by the supreme executive authority itself from time to time, over all the departments and executive officers employed in carrying into effect the laws and regulations intended to prevent abuse."

The report concludes with a statement of regulations which the committee would deem necessary, if ever the Coolie trade should be renewed. Into these we need not enter at present; suffice it to say, that they differ vastly from the provisions of the Colonial Passengers' Act. The committee candidly state that they framed their suggestions, "not without a hope" that, if they should be adopted, "the trade would be abandoned as unprofitable by all parties now engaged in it."

We learn from the report, that, of the six gentlemen who composed the committee, two were "favourable to the trade, and one actually engaged in it." These, no doubt, are the two dissidents. One of them, Mr. Dowson, has expressed his views in a minute appended to the report. He describes it as "a case got up against the Mauritius interests, in a spirit of the most reckless exaggeration!" This is the Coolie trader, beyond question; and staunch to the last.

No. IV.

From the Anti-Slavery Reporter, Oct. 20th, 1841.

SUBSEQUENTLY to the defeat of Lord John Russell's motion last year, to relax the prohibition laid by the Supreme Government of India, on the export of Coolies to Mauritius and elsewhere, in consequence of the fearful abuses which had attended the measure, and which all the police regulations they could devise had neither been able to correct or control, several important documents have been laid before parliament relative thereto, which fully justify the course which had been taken, and render it imperative that the prohibition should be continued.

The argument raised by the Mauritian planters, that the prohibition interferes with the rights of the Indian labouring population, is met by the fact, that that population, so far from desiring to emigrate from their native land to distant and foreign parts, are utterly averse to it. They even object to go to distant and unknown sections of their own country, although allured by the company's servants, under the promise of constant employment, good wages, land for tillage, and ample protection. We have an instance of this in a communication of Capt. T. Wilkinson, agent to the governor-general, south-western frontier, to N. Willich, Esq., secretary to the Tea Company, dated 20th February, 1839. Captain Wilkinson states, that after having informed the Coolies that if they would proceed to Assam for the cultivation of tea, "they would never receive less than three rupees per mensem, for their labour, and would be allowed land to cultivate, free of expense, for a period of five years, and have their travelling expenses to Assam paid at the rate of two rupees per mensem," states that they refused on the ground that they were not "willing to go to a country which they cannot ascertain has been visited by any of their brethren. They also expressed fears that I might be endeavouring to procure them to send them beyond sea, as several had been sent from Calcutta by gentlemen." Another of the company's servants, J. Davidson, Esq., in a letter to Dr. Wallich, dated 30th March, 1839, says that, his endeavours to obtain Coolies to go to Assam were "entirely without success," the idea that they "are willing to expatriate themselves is directly the reverse of the fact," as no people "are more attached to their own country than the Coolies, and with reason." It should also be observed, that, of all the thousands who have hitherto gone to Mauritius, or other colonies, there is no proof afforded that any of them went voluntarily; but, on the contrary, decisive evidence that they were either kidnapped for that purpose, and by force put on board vessels employed in transporting them, or were obtained by the most fraudulent statements, such as, that they were wanted for the "company's *rabustie;*" and that agency-houses in Calcutta, crimps and police, were all parties to the infamous transactions. Even the governor-general, who is now willing to relax the prohibition partially, observes in a minute, dated 25th April, 1841, "I do not believe that this law (the prohibitory act) is yet felt as pressing hardly upon the rights and interests of the natives of India." The fact is the law is protective merely—protective of the liberty and happiness of the Indian population, and it will certainly be time enough to repeal it when they feel it to be a grievance.

But the Mauritian planters want labourers to extend their cultivation and increase their riches, and they consider it an infringement of their rights to restrict the labour market to them, by a prohibitory law, having reference to Indian labourers. The reply to this is, that they shut that market themselves. They did not obtain the labourers by fair means, but by foul. The most atrocious practices were resorted to, year after year, by their agents in India, until the evil of their doings became so glaring, and monstrous, and incurable, that they were absolutely forbidden to resort thither for more victims to satisfy their love of gain. The rights of Mauritian planters! Men who never respected the rights of others, should be modest in speaking of their own. They should remember that the miserable remnant of labourers they impiously claimed as their property, up to the period when the abolition act delivered them from their oppressors, were the victims of an atrocious slave trade, carried on by themselves in defiance of all laws human and divine. They should remember that to them, belongs the bad pre-eminence of having resisted to the last the abolition of the apprenticeship, second only in horror to the system of slavery itself, and which they enforced by a more dreadful severity than by any other oppressors in the whole of the British colonies. They should remember that the Coolies they have already in possession were obtained by force or fraud, when they talk of their rights. Had they recruited their population in the first instance by honourable means—had they introduced the Indian labourers into their colony as free men, free to choose their own masters, and free to demand the current wages that were given—had they legislated in the spirit of the Abolition Act, to meet the altered state of the colony—had they treated their emancipated slaves with justice, the probability is, that, under proper restrictions, they would have been allowed a free resort to British India, for such additional labour as they might want; but on all these points they have shown that they are neither to be trusted by the British government nor by the British people; and they must take the consequences of their own acts.

But to return to the official papers referred to in the opening paragraph of this article.

1. The first, No. 331, 1840, contains " copies of correspondence addressed by the Secretary of State for the colonial department, relative to the introduction of Indian labourers into Mauritius; and of the report of the commissioners of inquiry into the present condition of those already located in the colony." From it we gather, that on twenty-two estates out of thirty, that were visited by the commissioners, serious complaints were made by the Coolies. It also appears by the same document, that out of 25,000 Coolies introduced in four years, 7,000 had perished ! In a previous parliamentary return, No. 58, 1840, the mortality at Port Louis was stated to be from 8 to 9 per cent. per annum, and that out of 19,050 Coolies which had then been introduced, only 205 were women ! In both these documents, it is proved that the generality of the abodes of the Coolies were wretched, that the hospital accommodations were, in most instances, abominable—that they were sometimes coerced to labour—that their services were transferred from one master to another, by *sale* for *a pecuniary profit*—that they were obliged to obtain a " *billet de passe*," to go beyond the estates to which they were attached during out-of-work hours—that they were mulcted *two days' wages for one day's absence*,—and were subject to various other " horrid abuses," to use the language of one of the gentlemen engaged in the examination.

2. The next parliamentary paper, No. 45, 1841, contains " copies of a letter from the secretary to the government of India, to the committee appointed to inquire respecting the export of Hill Coolies, dated 1st day of August, 1838; of the report made by the committee, with the minutes and appendix ; of any minute recorded on that report by any member of the committee; of the letters from the government of India to the Court of Directors of the East India Company, dated the 16th and 19th days of October, 1840, on the same subject." The evidence contained in this important document decided the government of India as to the course which it was bound in honour and humanity to pursue, and led to the prohibition so often referred to. In the report of the committee they say, " We

conceive it to be distinctly proved beyond dispute that the Coolies and other natives exported to Mauritius and elsewhere, were, generally speaking, induced to come to Calcutta, by misrepresentation and deceit, practised upon them by native crimps, styled duffadars and arkotties, employed by European and Anglo-Indian undertakers and shippers, who were mostly cognizant of these frauds, and who received a very considerable sum per head for each Coolie imported." " That kidnapping prevailed to a very considerable extent ; and the Coolies, while kept in Calcutta itself and its neighbourhood, were actually in a state of close imprisonment." " That whatever measures were adopted by the police were completely ineffectual as a check upon these abuses." " That the police regulations of Mauritius were of not much greater practical utility in restraining illegal importations of Coolies." " That the hardships and miseries endured by the Coolies in the passage to Mauritius, were very great ; and the mortality from drowning (suicide, &c.), and other causes, was most serious—not much short," they add, " of ten per cent. on the numbers exported." They then submit certain suggestions to the government to prevent abuses in future, in closing which they observe, " We have framed these suggestions, not without a hope that if our views of regulating to the full extent pointed out, shall be adopted, the trade would be abandoned as unprofitable by all parties now engaged in it. And we repeat, that while we are of opinion that even such laws as those would not be wholly effectual in extinguishing abuses, if the exportation of Coolies should be carried on in great numbers, yet we believe that, if adopted, it is unlikely that the exportation of Coolies would afterwards go on to any great extent, and then abuses might become manageable." The facts collected in the evidence were of the most painful kind. We need not dwell on them, as they are well known. One of the witnesses examined by the committee as to the condition of the Coolies in Mauritius, made the following remarkable statement, which proves that the planters are as opposed to the education of the wretched Coolies, as they were reckless of the means by which they obtained them. Mr. Onslow says, "I may mention, with reference to the civilization and well being of the Coolies, that means which had been taken to promote their spiritual welfare in Mauritius were, for some reasons, prevented from being carried into effect by, I believe, the government of Mauritius. An impression existed, I understand, that the preaching of missionaries had a tendency to render people of the class of Coolies discontented with their situation and their masters."

In concluding their valuable report, the committee observe, " We have a full trust that the benevolent and commanding intellects employed in the consideration of the whole subject in England, both in parliament and out of it, cannot fail to lead the legislature to right conclusions ; and we rest humbly confident in the conclusion that, whatever may be the result, parliament and the people of England will duly protect the emancipated African from all competition in the wages of labour and means of subsistence, that is not free, fair, and unaided by local power ; and will not permit injustice to be done to the Indian subjects of the crown (though of a poor and friendless class), from any motives of political advantage, however weighty, or of mercantile gain, however large."

3. The third series of documents printed by order of parliament, No. 427 (1841), contains "copy of Mr. J. P. Grant's minute on the abuses alleged to exist in the export of Coolies, and an appendix, containing the examination of Coolies returned from Mauritius to Calcutta. The object of Mr. Grant is to obtain the relaxation of the prohibition laid by the government of India on the export of Coolies to Mauritius, on the ground that the whole of the labouring population of the vast portion of her majesty's territories entrusted to the government of the East India company, ought to be as free as the rest of her majesty's subjects in respect to the disposal of their labour, and their right of going about." It is material, however, to observe, that Mr. Grant fully admits the correctness of the statements contained in the report of the committee, before adverted to, as to the manner in which the Coolie trade was carried on, the treatment of the labourers before embarkation, and the treatment to which they were generally subject in Mauritius. "In these particulars," Mr. Grant says, "so far from objecting to the opinions of the majority, if I had agreed in the conclusion of the report, and so been competent to sign it, I should have felt it my duty to move for a more pointed expression of opinion in certain respects." Notwithstanding, however, this important admission, he is the advocate for Coolie emigration to Mauritius under certain regulations which he proposes. He would limit the emigration to certain ports. At these ports he would have a protector of Indian emigrants. He would have the labourer fully understand what he undertakes. He would institute a registry of certificates granted. He would not allow the Coolies to be shipped in batches. He would give the Coolie the opportunity of changing his mind at any time previous to the sailing of the emigrant vessels. He would have security that the labourers should return to their native land. He suggests that a law of the imperial legislature would be necessary to ensure, on the part of the owners of vessels, obedience to such regulations as the Indian government might frame; and that, to prevent smuggling, British vessels every where might be liable to search by men-of-war, and subject to heavy punishment if found to have Coolies on board improperly obtained. He also recommends that permission might be refused by the government of India to ship emigrants to any colony (Bourbon, for instance) where the law applicable to emigrants is not in all respects such as is suitable to free men of that class. Other regulations, more or less stringent, to take effect in Mauritius, are suggested by Mr. Grant, and with such limitations and restrictions as he proposes he thinks the system may be permitted. How far his regulations qualify the proposition on which he bases his willingness to allow of emigration we will not stop to inquire. If his argument had reference exclusively to the spontaneous emigration of skilled labourers, whose acts were perfectly voluntary, we could understand it, but as he would apply it to the ignorant and unwary, we must say, with the facts before us, it is

perfectly inconclusive, and as to the regulations which he suggests, we think it sufficient to quote from the governor-general's minute of the 25th of April, 1841, the following extract, to show their inefficiency. His lordship says, " I greatly fear no strictness of regulation, and no vigilance on the part of the authorities, would immediately prevent the frequent infliction of grievous oppressions and deceits upon large numbers of persons helpless from their poverty, and from their ignorance and inexperience." It is to protect these that we advocate the continuance of the prohibition. And as to the police, to whose hands this matter must be left, his lordship adds, " It is but too true, that this branch of our service is most defective and ineffective, and the different experiments which have been tried for its reform have greatly ended in disappointment." But among the regulations of Mr. Grant, we do not find one that has reference to an equality of the sexes among the emigrants. We presume the reason for this will be found in the utter unwillingness of the female sex to leave their native homes. Yet it will, perhaps, not be improper to inquire what may become of the wives and children of emigrant Coolies, when their husbands and fathers are taken from them. In the appendix to the report of the committee, some light is thrown upon this subject. These gentlemen had been able to trace the history of many families after the departure of their relatives to Mauritius, and this is the melancholy account: "At present their families, for want of food, are begging from door to door"—"family is in great distress for maintenance"—"starving for want of food"—"their families have taken menial service (become slaves?) for maintenance." And these remarks are not confined to a family here and there, but are applicable to a great extent to all the families left at home by the Coolies on their shipment for Mauritius. Now, two evils are inflicted by the wholesale removal of males; first, the injury inflicted on the miserable families they leave behind; and, secondly, the demoralization they necessarily carry with them. To dwell on this point is unnecessary. The introduction of 30,000 or 40,000 males of the Mohammedan and idolatrous population of Hindostan into the midst of the labouring community of Mauritius—subject to none, or but few of those moral restraints which Christianity inculcates, must be an evil of frightful magnitude, in whatever point of view it be regarded.

In connexion with Mr. Grant's minute, we find the evidence of 123 Coolies, who have returned to Calcutta, after the expiry of their indentures. They were examined principally by Mr. M'Farlan, police magistrate, occasionally assisted by Mr. Grant, Mr. Dowson, and Russomoy Dutt, a native gentleman. The mode in which they were examined is extremely unsatisfactory. No uniformity in the questions proposed to the Coolies was observed, except to elicit what might be deemed favourable to the Mauritian planters, and to the scheme of emigration. In the examination, both Mr. Grant and Mr. M'Farlan show themselves decided partizans. As to Mr. Dowson, he was directly engaged in shipping Coolies to Mauritius, as may be seen by parliamentary papers 45 (1841), p. 75. In his deposition before the committee of inquiry, he admits that his house shipped 6000 Coolies to Mauritius, and 51 to Bourbon. This man pretended not to know how his subordinate agents obtained the Coolies, or whether they were confined by his duffadars previously to embarkation, but confessed that, on one occasion, he had 140 in his own compound, guarded by brijabassies for no purposes whatever, certainly not to prevent the Coolies from going whithersoever they pleased! It appears, however, that the great gates of the compound were always kept closed, and that after four or five weeks' confinement, the Coolies mutinied and fought their way out of the place, to the no small regret of Mr. Dowson, who had made some advances to them.

But to return to the evidence of the Coolies. The fact that they returned with money in their pockets, some after a residence of five years, and some after they had served a period of six years, with from 10 to 300 rupees each, is paraded in the examination as a most convincing proof of the excellent treatment they received. Now, an ordinary Coolie's wages, at five rupees per month, would amount to sixty rupees per year, and in five years to 300 rupees; whilst that of a sirdar or head servant, at seven to ten rupees per month, would of course be in proportion. In analyzing, however, the amount said to have been brought by 123 Coolies to Calcutta, we find the result to be as follows, viz. 26 with sixty rupees and under, 34 with 120 rupees and under, 23 with 180 rupees and under, 17 with 240 rupees and under, 17 with 300 rupees and under, 1 with 350 rupees, another 354 rupees, and a third 400 rupees; whilst three appear to have brought none away with them. Upon a close examination, we find that those with the larger sums were mostly the sirdars or headmen, or Coolies who had wives and children that could assist them in labour, or persons who added to their stock by trading, &c. It should also be observed, that in the sums brought home with them, was included the amount kept back, one rupee per month, as a deposit, in case they should become diseased or incorrigible, and be sent back to India before the expiry of their indentures. The test, however, we would apply, is their willingness to return to Mauritius. On this point the examinations give us the following results : three state they would go back—these were sirdars, or persons who had been instructed to bring labourers back to the Mauritius with them ; ten doubtful—perhaps they might go back, cannot tell whether they might go back, and such like answers ; eighteen would not return ; the remainder either gave no answers upon the point, or were not questioned. Among those who gave a decided negative, we find several who brought away the largest amounts of money. In their examinations the Coolies are almost invariably represented as having no complaints, and yet we find many among them making the following statements :—" They exact hard labour." " I was flogged for not working properly." " He was beat." " He was beat if he did not do his work." " We were occasionally beaten, but not after we learned our business." " We were allowed very little, only about three-eighths of a seer (of rice) a day." " We were told that we were engaged to do the company's work." "If they had not supposed they were going to serve the company they would not have gone." "On Sundays we did not work after eight o'clock in the morning." "On Sundays we got our week's rations." "At ten o'clock, A. M., we had an hour allowed to eat our dinners ; that was the only rest we were allowed in the day." "On Sundays, when we mixed with other Coolies, we heard complaints of ill-treatment from some—they complained that as a punishment their hands were tied behind them, and they were whipped with the mule whip, and their feet were put in stocks." "He (the sirdar) practised oppression upon us." "When we complained to the master, he used to say to him, that for not working we were beat.—He used to take bribes from us ; I paid two rupees three times to him." "After eight o'clock (on Sundays) we had a pass if we wanted to go out ; without a pass the police would stop us, and take us to the thannah." "Many of us would not work, and were beat." "We were beat when we did not work." "If I did not work I was locked up, and put in the stocks." "I (a brahmin) experienced great trouble at Mauritius." "Two days' pay were deducted for one day's leave." "I was promised clothes every six months, but I only got annual clothing." "If I was sick one day, two days' wages were cut." "I was occasionally beat for not working." "The work is hard even in the rains." "The sirdar used to administer the blows by order of the overseer." "We had hard work—we were made to work." "If I was slow at work, I used to get a slap on my posteriors with a cane," &c. &c. These incidental allusions will show the sort of treatment to which the Coolies were subjected in Mauritius ; and may well create a grave suspicion of the mildness of the system said to have been pursued towards the Coolies by the Mauritian planters.

4. The last parliamentary document presented to Parliament, No. 43 (1841), contains, among other matters, minutes on the export of Coolies to Mauritius, drawn up by the Governor-General, W. W. Bird, H. T. Prinsep, and A. Amos, Esqrs., and a communication dated the 15th of February, 1841, from the colonial secretary at Mauritius, to the secretary of the government of India, embodying the sentiments of Sir Lionel Smith on the same subject. In this despatch his excellency states, that the Coolies "have by no means been harshly dealt with, oppressed, or neglected ; and he is quite satisfied that the interests of the planters themselves, and the intelligence of the Indians in the modes of ensuring redress of wrongs which they habitually enjoyed under the company's servants in India, guarantee to them justice and good treatment from their employers in this island." To what are we to attribute this singular statement ? To age and infirmity ? The three things presented to our attention are, the good treatment of the employers, the intelligence of the Coolies, and the habitual justice meted out to natives of India by the company's servants ! Why, we have as much faith in the one as in the other. If the poor Coolies have not a better guarantee for good treatment than this, we fear they will never get it ! But Sir Lionel goes on to say, "he is quite satisfied that, with

a government like this, powerful enough to enforce the Queen's commands, even the most ill-disposed planters in this colony can be controlled, against the exercise of arbitrary or unjust power." Then what becomes of his excellency's experience in Jamaica? Is he stronger in Mauritius than he was in Jamaica? And what becomes of *our* experience of Mauritian honour, humanity, loyalty to the crown, and obedience to the laws? Sir Lionel is, we believe, stronger in confidence than in power, and he must pardon us when we say that even the pledge which he gives of his ability to keep the planters of Mauritius in order, is insufficient to convince us that he can do so, or that they are to be entrusted with the liberty and welfare of thousands of illiterate Hindoos. Mr. Amos, in his minute, observes, " I think it would be expedient to allow of the emigration of the natives of India to Ceylon, Mauritius, and BOURBON, under the following regulations :—I. The laws of these islands should provide for their protection during their period of contract, which should at first be limited, and for their return to India; and the possibility of these islands being made an entrepot for the shipment of Coolies to more distant and less regulated places should be carefully guarded against. 2. Rules should be enacted, providing for the health and comfort of emigrants on board ship. 3. The enactment of severe penalties against crimping, which may be extended to Lascars, and which should include false representations, especially the use of the pretended authority of government. 4. Perhaps a register should be kept." It may appear presumptuous in us to differ in opinion from so learned a man as Mr. Amos, but we really think, that unless he go much further than he states, his plan is a most inefficient one, and much less worthy of consideration than Mr. Grant's. Mr. Prinsep, the government secretary, " would not allow labourers to proceed at present beyond the Cape of Good Hope." He would require " that no labourer should be allowed to embark under contract for more than five years"—" a life contract should not be permitted, until we have full assurance that the labourer knows perfectly the kind of life, and labour, and the climate which he is binding himself to for ever." He would enact, " that whatever advances might be given as an inducement to embark, the labourer should not be bound for them after landing in the colony of his destination ;" that " every ship licensed, should have an officer of customs on board to the time of sailing, to take account of the labourers shipped," &c.; and that a " registry should be established." Mr. Prinsep, as well as Mr. Amos, would allow the Coolies to be taken to Bourbon. Mr. Bird entirely differs from these gentlemen, and would continue the prohibition, for many good and sufficient reasons. In reference to the prohibition itself, he says, " It was not resolved upon until repeated attempts, by means of regulation, to check the abuses that were being committed, had been made in vain : and it is impossible, I think, to doubt, after reading the evidence which has been adduced, that it is to this law alone we are indebted for a stop being put to a system of wholesale oppression, in which, with shame be it spoken, the police were deeply implicated, more disgraceful than any that the natives have experienced at the hands of Europeans in this country, for many years." He further observes—" The law, so far from being too stringent, would, I apprehend, have been of little use had it been less so, owing to the facilities which exist every where, for kidnapping and surreptitious shipment, whenever the temptation to practise it is sufficient to excite the cupidity of crimps and other miscreants who form the agency employed on such occasions." In replying to the objection that the prohibition interfered with spontaneous emigration, Mr. Bird says, "The disgraceful practices to which exporters have been obliged to resort, and of which, it must be supposed, they never would have been guilty, could the labourers have been procured by less exceptionable means, prove any thing but that they go of their own free-will ; and it may be affirmed, that to travel beyond sea, even for the purpose of bettering their condition, is an undertaking to which the natives of India are but little addicted. Not a single complaint against the prohibition from any individual, except the exporters alluded to, has been made since the law was passed ; and as for the Hill Coolies, so little are they disposed to emigrate to places beyond the confines of India, that when we were desirous, not long ago, of procuring a number of them to work in the tea plantations of Assam, the local authorities who were employed to obtain them failed entirely, because of their unwillingness to go to a country of which they knew nothing, and their fears of being sent, as others had been from Calcutta, beyond sea." Mr. Bird then asserts, that the number of Coolies required by the Mauritians, cannot be "obtained by fair means," and that "the question really is, whether by any thing short of prohibition, due protection can be afforded to the bulk of the native population, or to expose, for the sake of a few, the most defenceless portion of the native population, from being involuntarily taken from their homes and their families, to promote European objects in foreign countries." He has no objection whatever to allow "those who possess skill and enterprise," the liberty of emigrating, and this may be done "by merely reserving to the local government the power of granting permission in such cases," but he contends that it is not necessary to allow of free emigration to the bulk of the population, and thus give rise "to a renewal of all the abominations from which, by the law in question, they have so recently been rescued." In conclusion, Mr. Bird observes, "I do not place much reliance on the testimony of the Coolies who have lately returned from Mauritius." . . . "I am not satisfied," he adds, "with the summary manner in which their examinations have been taken by the chief magistrate, who appears throughout in the character of a partizan arguing in favour of the Coolie trade." Finally, he recommends that in the event of such renewed emigration, care should be taken to guard against giving the least countenance to a prescriptive claim to our labourers. The planters, he says, "having once obtained permission to procure them, would doubtless demand compensation for the deterioration of their estates, were the privilege of exporting them at any time to be withdrawn." And, Mr. Bird might have added, that, whilst the planters are allowed to import any amount of adult labourers they please to cultivate their estates, they never will care for rearing a Creole peasantry, nor pay that attention to human happiness, and to the social, moral, and religious well-being of the people, which a wise and humane policy on the part of the home government, and especially which the benign principles of Christianity render imperative on all who respect its claims.

The governor-general having also taken this important subject into consideration, gives a very qualified opinion on the expediency of re-opening the question of free emigration, as it is termed. His lordship candidly confesses that he has been led to no very satisfactory general conclusion upon it. However, he states that the law of prohibition " is most objectionable in principle ;" but he does not " believe *that this law is yet felt as pressing hardly on the rights and interests of the natives of India.*" " It was," Lord Auckland remarks, " upon no understood practice, and only through the busy intervention of an active agency, that the first emigrants were led to seek their fortunes in the Mauritius." To the perfectly voluntary emigration of industrious labourers his lordship has no objection, but in dealing with the particular case in hand, he feels great difficulty. He says, " Under ordinary circumstances, and if the slave trade and slavery had never been, we might, perhaps, approach the question of an open emigration with some hope of devising checks which might be relied on as generally effectual against abuse. But there is at present, in the sugar islands, a dearth of labour, which has so raised prices as to put in action every feeling of cupidity, with all the instruments by which labourers can be obtained. The number of labourers required is so great, that it could not be supplied by those only who could calculate the advantage of the change. Even for the well-understood contracts of the soldier or the sailor, it is known into what tricks and acts of violence the low, and sometimes the higher agent, are led ; and when, for the supply of thousands and thousands of labourers to various remote settlements, the iniquitous craft of this great city (Calcutta) finds its account in acting the crimp upon those who are simple and unguarded, I greatly fear that though amendment and caution would, no doubt, come with time, *no strictness of regulation, and no vigilance on the part of the authorities, would immediately prevent the frequent infliction of grievous oppressions and deceits upon large numbers of persons helpless from their poverty, and from their utter ignorance and inexperience.*" This passage contrasts very remarkably with the complimentary statement of Sir Lionel Smith, before referred to. Lord Auckland must have smiled when he read it. And as for the protection which the natives enjoy from the police regulations of India, what must the condition of the lower class of the population be, when his lordship states in reference to the police itself, " *It is but too true that this branch of our service is most defective and ineffective, and the different experiments which have been tried for its reform, have ended in disappointment.*" The police may form an admirable body of agents for the Mauritian planters, but this confession, wrung from his lordship, proves that they cannot be trusted with the liberties of the people, and that justice, at all events, is not to be expected at their hands. Lord Auckland is willing, however, to try the experiment once more with Mauritius, and he states that " by the appointment of a distinct ' protector' of emigrants, by the inspection and limitation of contracts, and the prohibition of money advances, and by the regulation of shipping, and the other rules proposed, we might, I think, do much," he says, " in the few ports from which emigration to the Mauritius might be limited, and for some stated number of emigrants, towards the entire suppression of the practices, of which three or four years ago there was too much reason to complain ;" and he adds, " We could at the same time always satisfy ourselves that the measures adopted in the Mauritius for the protection of the labourers, when on the island, are operative and sufficient." In further elucidation of his sentiments, his lordship observes, " We must remember, however, that in permitting emigration to Mauritius, it would be necessary to guard against the possibility of labourers shipped nominally for that island being carried elsewhere, or their being inveigled while on the island into contracts of service in other settlements, where we could have no security for their treatment." His lordship is suspicious of Bourbon. He says, " We cannot expect that we shall be permitted to stock Mauritius with labourers without immediate facilities being again given by the French authorities for emigration to Bourbon," through the settlement at Pondicherry. Without guarantees for the " steady enforcement of measures of effectual precaution and protection within their settlements," Lord Auckland says, " I fear we should not be justified in re-opening emigration even to Mauritius." Whatever difficulty his lordship may have felt in speaking out upon this subject, we have no hesitation in saying, that it is our assured belief, that the Coolies who have been exported to Bourbon, are to all intents and purposes slaves, whatever they may be nominally, and that to allow of their farther export, to that island, would be neither less nor more than permission to carry on the slave trade, of which British subjects would be the victims.

As a practical measure, Lord Auckland would so far relax the prohibition, as to permit the " skilful artizan, or the man of calculating enterprise," to emigrate. He would, therefore, adopt a regulation which should permit " ten or twenty such passengers, perhaps not more than one to twenty-five tons; to embark in vessels." " A provision of this kind would be open to none of the objections by which the adoption of a larger measure may be impeded, and it would take off its character of excessive and impolitic, if not unjust restraint, from the enactment as it at present stands."

With this concluding extract from Lord Auckland's minute, we bring our analysis of the parliamentary papers referred to in the opening paragraphs of this article to a close. We have taken pains to examine them minutely, and we have felt the importance of presenting their substance in a compact form to our readers, because, after all, the battle respecting Coolie emigration must be fought in England. Already the planters, and their agents in this country, have taken the field. Major Archer is home from the Mauritius, and has already advocated the scheme in a pamphlet, and in an insidious letter which has appeared in the columns of the *Times.* Mr. Grant is home. He is by far the most able and talented of their advocates, and on his exertions and influence with the government, the Mauritians greatly rely. Besides these gentlemen, there is the influential house of Barclay, Irving, and Co., ever watchful, ever active to forward the interests of the Mauritians, because their own is so completely bound up with them. We must counteract them. With us it must be a question not of emigration to Mauritius, or elsewhere, but of PROTECTION TO THE NATIVES OF INDIA. We must prevent their being sacrificed, nay, of their sacrificing themselves, to the all-devouring spirit of cupidity.

The following are extracts from the East India papers on the subject referred to in the preceding article :—

COOLIE EMIGRATION.

" The *Eastern Star* holds forth an argument in favour of the Coolie trade, which we cannot suffer to pass without observation. The Mauritius planters have opened what our contemporary thinks ' *must inevitably be a slave-trade,*' and, therefore, he would permit (the so-called) *voluntary* emigration of Indian labourers. We know that some heterodox moralists have urged that houses of ill fame ought to be tolerated in cities as a safety valve for the licentious passions of the multitude, and consequently as a protection to the virtuous part of the female community. But we never yet heard it contended that because such houses are evils, the wives and daughters of the citizens should be given up to infamy, to prevent the necessity of permitting such establishments. But this is precisely the argument of the *Eastern Star.* The Mauritius planters will have labour at all events; they care not for the laws of God or man; felony and piracy are disregarded by them in the attainment of their object. Therefore, to prevent the renewal of these horrors, give up the inoffensive Indian labourer to the tender mercies of the kidnapper! We should have drawn an opposite conclusion from such premises. We do not accuse the planters of any wrong intention in their present attempt to procure labour; we have not facts before us to warrant an unfavourable conclusion. But had we grounds to believe with our contemporary that this is the commencement of a new slave-trade, we should have felt ourselves furnished with the strongest possible argument in favour of existing restrictions. We should have said at once, these people cannot be trusted with the control of an ignorant and uncivilized race; they are themselves but half reclaimed. Like Robinson Crusoe's man Friday, they have still the old hankering after human flesh, and every new attempt to obtain it ought to be a fresh caution to the legislature not to yield to their importunities.

" One word as to *voluntary* emigration. Will any British journalist deliberately assert that these poor people understand the nature of the contract into which they enter, or of the service into which they are going? Those who have returned, are the few who have saved money; who are of course tolerably satisfied with the result, whatever they may have been with the course of their labours. Yet even these few assert that flogging is the usual practice to compel labour on the estates. We maintain, that whenever an employer has power to compel work by corporeal punishment, the labourer is a slave. It is useless to allege military service, for there the officer is in the place of the civil power of the state. Its authority is delegated to him for a special purpose, and by that purpose it is limited. But there is no more reason (except a slave code) why a planter should be permitted to flog his labourers than a householder in Calcutta should be permitted to flog the same labourers before their embarkation. Mr. M'Farlan, who cannot now see any great objection to the trade, would fine a master in Calcutta one hundred rupees for a few slight blows given in anger and under provocation. Yet he cannot see the objection to the cat of nine tails, when in the hands of the planter, where no means of redress can be obtained for the unfortunate labourer ;— we were going to say—slave."—*Calcutta Englishman*, April 5th, 1841.

THE COOLIE TRADE.—" It is with deep—nay the deepest regret, that we have learnt that Lord Auckland has by the last despatch forwarded a minute to the home authorities recommendatory of the Coolie trade. His lordship's career has been hitherto one marked by a succession of successful events, if not for the exchequer of the company, at least for the honour of Britain. We regret, therefore, that he should have recommended one single measure which strikes so effectually at the root of the liberty of our poor deluded fellow-subjects in India. We know not how far his lordship's opinion may have been formed on Mr. Grant's minute, with which the public have just been favoured. This minute is the most able document which has yet appeared on the subject, and had it been penned to recommend the emigration of the destitute at home, we should have said it is admirably calculated to convince gainsayers. It is this very feature in it, however, that we have to lament in the present instance. The conclusions and reasonings are admirable, but the premises are wrong. Mr. G. sets out by begging the whole question in debate, viz., by assuming that the Coolie does understand the nature of the engagement into which he is entering, and that the advocates for the suppression of the trade, with the best intentions, strike at the root of the principle they profess to defend—the liberty of the subject; nay, that they in effect say to the Coolie, you shall not go where you please. That the Coolie does not understand the nature of his engagement is admitted by *all*. We have never heard a dissenting voice on this point—he cannot; it is an impossibility in the nature of things. We may as well talk of Mr. Grant comprehending an engagement to have and hold lands in some particular districts of the moon. The Coolie knows as much—nay less of this world, than Mr. G. or any other intelligent man does of the moon. That the friends of the Coolies have ever had the least wish to prevent their bettering their condition by removal to spots even more prophetic of good to them, we defy all the Coolie agents in the world to prove; but they have not been and cannot be convinced that to commit men helpless and ignorant into the hands of cunning and arbitrary men,

the old slave proprietors of the Mauritius, is either the way to im-
prove their moral and physical good, or to secure their liberty. Did
the Coolie know, was he aware of the true character of his future
employers and employment, we know enough of him to say, without
the fear of contradiction, that he would not go. The whole force of
Mr. Grant's minute rests upon these two fallacies; therefore if they
be disproved, the whole of its reasoning and recommendations must
fall to the ground. The writer has proceeded to Britain, and will
doubtless recommend in person this new slave-trade. This, together
with the minute of the governor-general, and the influence of the
slavery party, we fear will be but too likely to succeed. Our fears are
great—our hopes small. Should the trade be sanctioned, we shall see
the British Parliament placed in one of the most extraordinary posi-
tions in which any legislature can be placed. With the one hand she
has given twenty millions to remunerate the sugar planters from any
prospective losses arising out of the emancipation measure; while
with the other she is, in answer to the demands of these very so re-
munerated planters, about to allow them to carry off a race of people,
who will labour for them under the name of free men for slave wages,
to the great injury of the emancipated negroes and the new slaves :—
with the one hand she is sending out an expedition at a cost of
£20,000 to civilize Africa, with a view to the suppression of slavery all
over the world; while with the other she is peopling her colonies
under legal sanction with a new order of slavery. The battle must
now be fought in Britain."—*Christian Advocate,* April 24, 1841.

No. V.

ANALYSIS OF THE MOST RECENT PAPERS LAID BEFORE PARLIAMENT

ON THIS SUBJECT, &c. &c.

March 1, 1842.

AFTER the decision of the Supreme Government of India, in 1838,
against the export of Coolies to Mauritius and elsewhere, and the
decided negative put upon the proposal of Lord John Russell, to relax
the prohibition (under certain limitations and restrictions) in June,
1840, by the House of Commons, we must be allowed to express our
surprise that the noble lord, at present at the head of the Colonial
department, should have determined to open the trade once more,
and thus to disappoint the just expectations of the friends of
humanity, both in this country and in British India. It ought not
to pass without observation, that, while Lord John Russell allowed a
public discussion of the measure, before any steps were officially
taken, and gave an opportunity for the expression of public opinion

and the sense of the legislature, Lord Stanley has pursued a very different course.

At the time when Lord John Russell made his proposition to the House of Commons, the country was destitute (to a very great extent) of official information as to the reasons which had induced the Indian government to pass the prohibitory act, but parliamentary papers, since printed, Nos. 43 and 45, 1841, have fully justified the step which was then taken. The information which has been subsequently obtained, and on which it appears Lord Stanley grounds his measure for the repeal of the Prohibitory Act, will be found in Par. Paps. Nos. 66 and 427, 1841, and No. 26, 1842. The first of these documents contains correspondence relative to the introduction of Indian labourers into Mauritius, including report of proceedings in cases of assault, from 1st Jan. to 30th Sep., 1840 ; the second, Mr. Grant's Minute on the abuses said to exist in the export of Coolies to Mauritius, &c.; and the third, a continuation of the correspondence relative to the introduction of Indian labourers into Mauritius. How far these documents will bear out the government in the step they have taken, we shall now proceed to examine.

We may concede to Lord Stanley, that " it is requisite that no unnecessary discouragement should be given to the introduction of free labourers into our colonies ;" but we cannot agree with him in considering " the abolition of slavery " in the light of " an experiment, whether the staple products of tropical countries can be raised as effectually and as advantageously by the labour of freemen, as by that of slaves." That great measure was an act of justice—of bare justice—to a long-oppressed and suffering race, and was so regarded by the people and the legislature of this country. To treat it as "an experiment" is to lower the moral dignity of the act, and to measure its value by hogsheads of sugar and bags of coffee, rather than by the privations, sufferings, and degradation it has removed, the waste of human life it has prevented, and the freedom, civilization, and happiness it has conferred upon nearly a million of human beings, and their posterity for ever. No one knows better than Lord Stanley that the system of slavery in the British colonies was as impolitic as it was unjust ; no one more eloquently denounced it as such. It was in consequence of this conviction that, in the preamble of the law which abolished slavery, he caused to be inserted the memorable words—" it is just *and expedient* that they [the slaves] should be manumitted and set free."

The first document referred to (No. 66, 1841) contains a despatch from Sir Lionel Smith, dated the 29th December, 1840; in which, after treating the subject in a very loose and unsatisfactory way, he says, " I am of opinion the remedy for all the evils we are now suffering, or a means of improving the conduct of masters and labourers to each other, of putting down the temptations to wrong for the chances of higher wages, and to give just encouragement to agriculture, is to grant all possible facilities for an increase of labourers, and to receive as many here as can find employment, under protective regulations." In this extract we have a plea for the planters ; Sir Lionel would

" give just encouragement to agriculture " by an unlimited importation of labourers. In the following extract, taken from the same
despatch, we find a plea for the Coolies. " I will not close my letter
by promising that no injustice or oppression can possibly occur to the
Indians : but I will say, come what will, they will be infinitely better
off here, than in their own overstocked country, and that their mer-
cenary habits will be gratified, to the ultimate advantage of India and
Mauritius." Now we must be permitted to say, that, in both these
paragraphs, there is a large amount of assertion and very little proof.
Stripped of that which is mere opinion, all that Sir Lionel says comes
to this : " It is certainly very important to the planters of this
(colony), that they should know what they might expect in regard
to the supply of labourers from India, so as to regulate, for the ensuing
year, the sugar cultivation ; for, though they might find in the colony
sufficient labour to plant, they certainly would not have sufficient to
gather in crop, should it be at all extended, or even equal to past
years." This extract from another despatch of Sir Lionel Smith's, dated
24th February, 1841, places the matter on its true footing. *It is a
planters' affair altogether.* The guarantee we have that it shall work
no ill to the immigrants, is to be found in " protective regulations "
to be framed in India, and in the ability of Sir Lionel to give " full and
efficient protection " in Mauritius. As though, however, he had promised too much, he says, " I do not pretend to say that there will be
no abuse ; but I can answer for oppression and injustice being
punished in a way to put a stop to them, whenever any act of the
kind may become known." One might have imagined, that the experience of this veteran in colonial affairs, would have taught him to
speak less confidently on this point. He has to contend with men,
who, to use his own emphatic words, " are still mourning over the
loss of their slaves ;" and we fear, that if he could add the energies
of youth to the experience of age, the Mauritian planters would be
more than a match for him.

In connexion with the despatch of the 29th of December, 1840,
Sir Lionel Smith transmitted to the government an extended report
of proceedings in cases of assault, from the 1st of January to the
30th of September, 1840; with a view of showing that " many ac-
cusations against masters were totally unfounded, that a great many
others were frivolous, and that those which were found just, were
sufficiently punished." We should have been better pleased if this
report had comprehended also the offences, alleged to have been committed by the Coolies, against their employers, together with the
punishments inflicted upon them ; and still more satisfied, had the
returns embraced a larger period of time. From an analysis of the
return, such as it is, we find the planters or employers of Coolies
charged with about 480 assaults, sometimes aggravated by violation
of contract, non-payment of wages, refusing food, clothing, medical
treatment, illegal imprisonment, &c. &c. In about 235 cases the
masters or other defendants were convicted, and fined in various sums
from one shilling to ten pounds sterling. In 33 cases the complainants
were punished, either on counter charges brought against them by

their employers, or from their complaints being deemed vexatious, and sentenced to punishments, varying from three to fourteen days' imprisonment, with hard labour, mulcts of wages, &c. The rest of the cases were dismissed, either from want of sufficient evidence, or because the evidence was contradictory, or because the complainants were alleged to have given provocation to the assault. An attentive perusal of the returns of the different magistrates will show a decided leaning, on the part of many of them at least, towards the planters, and a determination (by the summary mode in which they dealt with the cases before them) to discourage the complaints of the Coolies. Indeed, one of the magistrates, Mr. Elliott, avows this. He had inflicted a fine of five rupees for an assault on a Coolie, which fine he gave to the " caisse de bienfaisance" (the charity fund), contrary to law. His motive for doing so, he thus explains : " I am aware that such is a deviation from the strict letter of the law, yet I considered it my duty, to prevent unjust complaints and discourage insubordination, to give a different direction to the fine. Cases of this nature are evidently *oversights by the legislature,* as it could never have been its intention to encourage complaints and discontent by a premium." The assault was proved, and the law provided that the injured party should receive the fine inflicted ; the magistrate, however, gives an illegal direction to it, and justifies his doing so on the ground of discouraging complaints and insubordination ! We may well suppose, that such a magistrate would dismiss all cases that came before him, unless the proof was of the strictest character ; and such, by a reference to his report, we find his practice to have been. Nor in this does he stand alone, as may be seen in the report of Mr. Heyliger, who appears on many occasions to have required the exhibition of marks of violence on the persons of the complainants as proof of an assault. Another mode of discouraging complaints may be illustrated from the report of Mr. Thatcher. It appears that an Indian labourer, of the name of Harlin, brought a complaint against Mr. Salesse for having beaten him. The assault was proved, but " Mr. Salesse deposed that he was obliged to speak to the complainant for neglect of work, when the complainant followed him (not very likely), and that he did strike him to relieve himself of him :" whereupon Mr. T. fined Mr. Salesse two shillings sterling for the assault, and sentenced Harlin to fourteen days' confinement with hard labour !" We beg to state that the words "not very likely," inserted in the above quotation, form part of the original record ; and yet such was his decision. We now call attention to the mode in which Mr. Regnard decided, in matters of complaint brought before him. One Vellaidon, sirdar in the service of Mlle. Gondreville, brought a charge of assault against Edgar Gondreville. The witnesses proved that Gondreville seized Vellaidon by the neckcloth, and shook him. This was not denied, but it was stated by Gondreville, in his defence, that Vellaidon had caused disorder among the Indians, and that at the time he did it, he was proceeding with certain Malabards, under his orders, to the police office ; whereupon the magistrate rejected the complaint of the sirdar, sentenced him to fourteen days' imprisonment with hard labour, and dismissed him from the situation of sirdar, which he said he was "unworthy to fill." In the record of Mr. Hervey we have the following case, illustrative of his practice : Shakismal, an Indian labourer, charged his master, M. Genave, with having refused to give him medicine when sick, and with locking him up in a chamber, adjoining the hospital, for a space of twenty-four hours. He failed to prove the first part of his complaint, but "M. Genave acknowledged having ordered him to be locked up, in consequence of his excessive insolence to him ;" whereupon Mr. Hervey *admonished* M. Genave, " for not immediately acquainting me of his being obliged to confine the Indian, Shakismal, for insolence to him ; and condemned the Indian, Shakismal, for giving a false statement, to eight days' imprisonment !" Other instances of a similar kind might be adduced, but we think these will be sufficient to show both the spirit and the mode, in which the laws of Mauritius are administered by the magistracy, and will account, in a great measure, for the number of complaints dismissed.

We gather from incidental remarks and complaints, that, in addition to the usual labour exacted from the Coolies during the week, they are expected to perform " corvée," i. e. a job, for the estate, on Sunday mornings, which, it appears, occupies them two or three hours : that, in some cases, a tribute is paid to the overseer of one rupee per month, to prevent ill-treatment ; and that many, if not all, the estate hospitals, are prisons in which the labourers are confined for various reasons, as under slavery. Whilst adverting to this latter point, we deem it necessary to call attention to the remarks of Mr. Kelly, stipendiary magistrate, on the general character of these places, and the necessity of some measure being adopted to correct the evils of which he complains ; he says, " The hospital accommodation and attendance generally afforded on estates to the sick, are so very defective in all those essentials, so necessary to the comfort and wants of the ailing, that I would submit the absolute necessity of some local measures, calculated to amend the present system. I am of opinion that, until private hospitals on estates are altogether abolished, and district hospitals erected, superintended by medical officers appointed by government, the desired object can never be realized." The neglect of the diseased and the treatment of the sick appears, in some cases, to be of the worst kind. (Vide pp. 58, 62, 84, 97.)

In this paper there remain only one or two points requiring notice. The first refers to the practice of deducting from the monthly wages of the Coolies one rupee, to form a fund, to enable them to return to India after the expiration of their contracts. An ordinance has been passed (No. 5 of 1840) declaring that " every person employing Indian servants is bound to furnish a security, to guarantee the payment of the sum retained from the wages of the labourers, and of the amount of the passage money for the return passage to India ;" and " in case of refusal, to furnish security, that the sum kept back, together with the amount of the return passage, shall be paid over to the treasury." This law is considered " a valuable boon to the labourers;" but, like many laws passed in the colonies, it has no executory principle. It does not point out the way in which masters can be compelled to refund the moneys they may retain, and is therefore little better than waste paper. We think that a rigid inquiry should be instituted, with a view of ascertaining what has become of the money retained by the planters, as well as of the wages that might have been due to Coolies who died before their contracts had terminated—a mere act of justice to the surviving relations of the deceased. The second point has relation to the proceedings of the Free-Labour Association established in Mauritius. It appears that their plans have met with the approbation of the Governor, who thinks, that, in the event of the Home and Indian Governments rescinding the prohibitory act, their proposals " could be easily embodied in a government ordinance, as experience or better information may show to be necessary." The scheme of the parties forming this association will be found in Par. Pap. No. 26, 1842, pp. 29 and 30. It is not necessary, however, to point out its defects, inasmuch as it is superseded by the plan which Lord Stanley intends should take effect.

Having given elsewhere * an abstract of the second document (No. 427, 1841) referred to, at the commencement of this review, it only remains for us to notice the last of the series (No. 26, 1842).

From two despatches from Sir Lionel Smith to Lord John Russell, dated the 7th of July and the 14th of August, 1841, it appears that there have been introduced into Mauritius, since the prohibitory law was enacted in British India, 815 Chinese from Penang and Sincapore, 650 natives of Madagascar, and 202 persons from the Comoro Islands,—in all 1667. Besides this, it appears " that, recently, two distinct attempts have been made by persons residing at Pondicherry to evade the provisions of that law, by sending agricultural labourers to the Island." Sir Lionel does not state the number (probably very small) of persons attempted to be introduced in this manner. With respect to the emigrants from Penang, Madagascar, and Comoro, the Governor, having ascertained that they had come willingly to the colony, allowed them to remain and engage themselves to any master they might choose. With respect to Pondicherry, it appears he has taken measures to prevent any more coming from that quarter, until the restriction shall be withdrawn.

The next point to be noticed in this paper is, the reply of the Free-Labour Association to a Report made by three of the gentlemen, appointed by the Supreme Government of India, to inquire into the abuses alleged to exist in the emigration of Indian labourers to the British Colonies. The object of this laboured attempt, is, of course, to disparage their valuable Report. Looking at the general character of the reply, and the bad spirit in which it is written, we much marvel that the government should have allowed it to appear. The gentlemen who form the Free-Labour Association at Mauritius, commence their attack on the Report by impeaching the motives of those

* Anti-Slavery Reporter, vol. 2 (1841), p. 225.

who made it, and by adverting to the circumstance that it was signed by three only out of the six gentlemen originally appointed to make the inquiry. This arose from one of them, Major Archer, having left Calcutta pending the inquiry, and two others, Messrs. Grant and Dowson, differing in opinion on some points, on which account they made separate reports, which have been printed. Major Archer, it would also appear, has published one or more pamphlets, expressing his opinions, but, not having seen them, we are not able to judge of their merits; if, however, their general tone be similar to the quotations given in the paper before us, we should attach but little importance to them. Mr. Grant, in his separate report, fully admits the correctness of the statements of the Committee of Inquiry, as to the manner in which the Coolie trade was carried on, the treatment of the labourers before embarkation, and subsequently to their arrival in Mauritius. " In these particulars," he says, " so far from objecting to the opinions of the majority, if I had agreed in the conclusion of the report, and so been competent to sign it, I should have felt it my duty to move, for a more pointed expression of opinion in certain respects." As to Mr. Dowson, whose evidence is quoted so triumphantly, he was a large shipper of Coolies, and, on one occasion at least, his agents in Calcutta locked up and strictly guarded, on premises belonging to himself, a considerable number of them, who had been improperly obtained, and who were subsequently liberated by the police. Before the gentlemen, whose names are attached to the reply, had ventured to attack the respectable persons who drew up the report, they should have remembered the position in which they stand. They are deeply interested in Coolie immigration, and, whatever value they may attach to their own opinions, they must be regarded only in the light of partisans, who are anxious either to conceal facts of a disgraceful nature, or to palliate them, when concealment is impossible. We do not think it necessary to examine their reply at length, or to place in juxta-position with their flippant assertions and remarks the heart-rending statements which they are unable to refute; we shall therefore dismiss it with a single quotation (given by themselves) from the pamphlet of their favourite advocate, Major Archer. He says, " It is admitted that the Indian labourers were, in numerous instances, deceived, defrauded, and most cruelly treated." Again, " The atrocities commenced in Calcutta, were, in some instances, continued during the voyage to Mauritius, or perhaps their effects were then felt with keener feelings, and under an inability to withstand them; some of these unfortunate individuals, who found themselves deceived, and unable to bear up against their misery, threw themselves overboard." He then adds, " If the regulations necessary for the emigration of Indian labourers had been as well understood and as fitting at Calcutta, as were the colonial laws passed on the occasion at Mauritius, I do not scruple to aver that the public would not have had its just indignation roused at the recital of such detestable atrocities." If! How much depends on an if! The regulations were stringent enough, but they were inoperative; and this we believe will be the case, with any regulations that may be

67

devised. As to the treatment of the Coolies in Mauritius, we have
no occasion to do more than to refer to the evidence already before
the public, and simply to remind our readers, that, on the testimony
of Mr. Anderson, who was selected by this very Free-Labour Association to represent them in England, the mortality of the Coolies,
when subjected to the tender mercies of the Mauritians, amounted,
in Port Louis, to from eight to nine per cent., whilst, in the country
districts, it ranged as high as from ten to eleven per cent. per annum,
being equal to the dreadful mortality of the slave population in Cuba!

We now come to the scheme of Lord Stanley, which has for its
object the introduction of Indian labourers into Mauritius, and the
outline of which he gives in his despatch to Sir Lionel Smith, dated
22nd of January, 1842. Passing over the noble lord's attempt to
meet some of the objections urged against the emigration of Coolies
to Mauritius, we wish to correct one or two material errors into
which he appears to have fallen. His lordship says, that "many of
those (the Coolies) who have already fulfilled their contracts in Mauritius have returned to India, and, having visited their families, and
deposited with them the amount of their accumulations, would gladly
enter into fresh engagements, were they not debarred by the existing
laws." We find no evidence of this in the documents laid before
parliament. With the exception of the three sirdars, to whom reference has been made elsewhere,* we can find none who were positively
willing, none who were anxious, as the noble lord would make it
appear, to return to Mauritius; and, if we may believe the Governor-
general of India, Mr. Bird, one of the council, Capt. Wilkinson, agent
of the Governor-general on the south-western frontier, or J. Davidson,
Esq., another of the Company's servants,—so far from there being
any desire, there is a manifest reluctance, on the part of the Indian
population generally, to emigrate to foreign lands. The proposed
repeal of the prohibitory act, therefore, cannot be grounded on the
wish of the native population of India to leave their homes; it must
rest entirely on the desire of the Mauritian planters to obtain them.

The noble lord further says, "It is evident from the report of Sir
Lionel Smith, that the urgency of the demand is triumphing over the
mere legal obstacles which interdict immigration; and that therefore, the existing law must be made more stringent, or relaxed."
Here again, we say there is no official evidence yet before the public
in support of this statement; on the contrary, Sir Lionel Smith states
that, in the case of the emigrants attempted to be introduced in con-
travention of the prohibitory act through the French settlement of
Pondicherry, he has taken effectual measures to prevent it in future.

Disapproving, as we do, of the whole measure, on grounds which
we shall presently state, we may be permitted, nevertheless, to remark on some of its highly objectionable details.

We deeply regret to perceive that Lord Stanley has not thought
fit to insist that, of the Coolies in future to be introduced into Mauritius, there shall be a due proportion of the sexes. All that his

lordship says upon this vital point is, that, "among the regulations thus to be established [by the Indian Government] will *probably* be such as may be requisite for maintaining a due proportion of sexes, and for the prevention of the improper separation of families, or the desertion of helpless women and children."* Why should that be left to probability which ought to be made peremptory? Sir Lionel Smith states, that the Coolies, already introduced, "have given themselves up to a degree of disgraceful licentiousness, which no person acquainted with their character and habits in India (dissolute as they are known to be) could possibly believe." Will the government sanction the increase of an evil so revolting as this, by the further introduction of any disproportionate number of males? Will not the House of Commons again interpose to prevent this and other enormous evils connected with Coolie emigration?

In the schedule, which accompanies the order in council, we find no provision made for a medical man to accompany the emigrants from India to Mauritius. This, for a voyage of from three to five weeks, we judge to be a most material omission. In the regulations for the supply of water and food to the emigrants during their voyage, we find that his lordship requires a supply of water to the amount of five gallons per week, and of rice, bread, biscuit, flour, oatmeal, or bread-stuffs, to the amount of seven pounds weight per week of the computed voyage, for every passenger, or the substitution, by the Governor-general of India, of any other articles of food, being in his judgment equivalent thereto. On this arrangement we have to remark, that the quantity of water should be at least one gallon *per diem* for each passenger, and that the amount of food is wholly inadequate to the proper support of life. If his lordship had consulted the schedule of the Free-Labour Association, he would find the following scale of rations as the daily allowance of Indians above ten years of age, viz. :—rice, 1 lb. 10 oz. avoirdupois, dholl or salt fish, 3 oz., ghee, $\frac{1}{2}$ oz., salt, $\frac{1}{4}$ oz. ; and if he compares this with the amount of food provided for the Coolies in Mauritius, he will find it to be little more than half the quantity considered necessary for their subsistence there, the average being $1\frac{3}{4}$ lbs. of rice *per diem*, with other articles in proportion. We trust his lordship will feel it his duty, should his plan come into operation, greatly to enlarge his scale, and to add to the rice or bread-stuffs such condiments as may be necessary to render them at all events palatable. We venture to suggest also to the noble lord, the necessity of providing that the food taken on board, for the use of the emigrants, shall be of good merchantable quality.

Although we have made these remarks on the details of Lord Stanley's plan, we must not be considered as approving it in its general features. Our objections to the entire measure remain in full force.

No one, who is at all informed upon the subject, can pretend that the natives of India have any wish to resort to Mauritius, however

---

* For particulars on these subjects see *Anti-Slavery Reporter.*

deplorable their condition may be in some extensive districts at home. The assertion that they would be generally benefited by the measure we deny. There is not a superabundant population in British India; and we venture to think, that, were a series of enlightened, humane, and comprehensive laws, substituted for those which now exist, and the present system of misgovernment abandoned, much would be done towards removing the misery which prevails in that country. Neither can any one pretend that the Mauritian planters are persons to whom the welfare of the Coolies may be safely entrusted. Their history is too well known to the people of this country to permit the expectation that they will treat them with humanity and justice. Even Sir Lionel Smith, who is quoted as an authority by Lord Stanley for his measure, says, in reference to them, " I have seen too much of the sacrifice of human life and human happiness in the production of sugar, to enable me to confide heartily in a class of men, allied so recently to such frightful systems," and " still mourning over the loss of their slaves."

In conclusion, we earnestly call upon the legislature to pause before they give their sanction to Lord Stanley's scheme, or allow themselves to be led away by the idea, that it is required as an act of justice to our Indian population. Let them remember that the destiny, for weal or woe, of multitudes of their fellow-men depends upon their decision. Above all, let them remember that it is their duty to protect the ignorant against the wiles of the crafty, the helpless against the strength of the powerful, the poor against the cupidity of the rich; and, by their responsibility to God as well to man, let them decide justly in this important matter.

Memorial to the Right Honourable Lord Stanley, &c. &c. from the British and Foreign Anti-Slavery Society.

My Lord,

The Committee of the British and Foreign Anti-Slavery Society have learned with deep regret, that it is the intention of Her Majesty's Government to relax the restrictions, at present in force in British India, against the export of Hill Coolies and other Indian labourers, so far as Mauritius is concerned, and to allow free importation of that class of persons into that island.

The Committee are aware that your Lordship intends, by certain regulations, to take effect in India, and on the voyage thence to Mauritius, to guard against some of the frightful evils which accompanied the introduction of Indian labourers into that colony previous to the passage of the Prohibitory Act in 1839; but they would respectfully observe to your Lordship, that nothing which has transpired since that period has reconciled them to the measure which your Lordship proposes should be adopted, and which, if carried into effect, they

B *

believe will be accompanied by evils far greater than appears to be contemplated, or against which it will be possible to guard.

Were the object of the measure recommended by your Lordship to secure to the labouring population of India a right which had been unwisely or unjustly taken from them, the Committee trust they would be found among its most earnest and zealous supporters; but when they perceive that its necessary consequence is, to withdraw that protection which the Supreme Government of India judged to be absolutely necessary to guard them from impositions the most fraudulent, and treatment the most cruel, they feel it to be their duty to take the earliest opportunity of expressing to your Lordship their decided objection to the proposed revocation of the existing law.

The Committee would venture to remind your Lordship, that what the Indian Government conceived to be necessary, the House of Commons, in the session of 1840, affirmed to be so, by a decided vote taken on the proposition of your Lordship's predecessor in office, which was similar to that now before the country.

Subsequently to that period, a large amount of official evidence on the subject of Coolie emigration has been laid before Parliament, which not only convinces the Committee of the wisdom and humanity of the course pursued both in India and in England on the subject, but which confirms them in the opinion, that, under present circumstances, there ought to be no relaxation in the restrictions which exist, except, perhaps, in the case of skilled labourers or artizans, who, on their own proper account, may desire to emigrate to other countries to better their condition.

Your Lordship's measure appears to be grounded on the fact, that in Mauritius "a constant and large demand for labour exists;" on the alleged charge that the emancipated slaves "are addicted to idle, vagrant, and unprofitable habits;" on the assumption that "many (of the Coolies) who have already fulfilled their contracts in Mauritius, have returned to India, and having visited their families, and deposited with them the amount of their accumulations, would gladly enter into fresh engagements, were they not debarred by the existing law;" and on the opinion which your Lordship entertains of being able to guard against abuses by certain regulations intended to be enforced in connexion with the emigration of labourers from British India.

On the first point, the question may arise, whether there be not a sufficient supply of labour in Mauritius to keep up, and gradually to extend, the sugar cultivation of the colony. The Committee are not convinced that there is not; but even if they were, they must protest against that being considered a sufficient ground for the introduction of Indian labourers into it. Labour is wanted in other British colonies for the same purpose, but your Lordship very properly, as they think, refuses them that which it is intended shall be granted to Mauritius.

In reference to the alleged charge of indolence, brought against the emancipated classes, they have yet to be convinced of its truth; but if it were true, that there is an unwillingness on their part to work for the planters, the Committee think that it may be found to originate in other causes than those laid to their account, namely, the past conduct of their masters, which, by the returns made to parliament, is proved to have been more fraudulent, cruel, and atrocious than that of any other slave colony of the crown; and the supercession of their labour, by that of the Coolies brought into the colony, under contracts for lengthened periods of time, at extremely low wages, under the pretence of the exorbitant demands of the negroes, and the attempt thus to coerce them. If, after having been driven from the land they formerly cultivated as slaves, they engage in desultory labour only, the Committee are persuaded that the cause will be found lying at the planters' door, rather than at theirs, and forms no just ground, in their judgment, why Indian labourers should be introduced into that colony.

But it is assumed, that the Indian labourers who have returned home with their earnings, are desirous of renewing their engagements in Mauritius, which they are debarred from doing under existing laws. So far as the papers already laid before parliament refer to this point, it does not appear that many are willing to return to the scene of their former labours, but the contrary. Three only positively state their intention to return, and these are sirdars, and were evidently sent to Calcutta rather as decoys, than as truthful witnesses of what they knew to be the actual condition of the labourers in that colony. Adverting to this point, Mr. Bird, of the Supreme Council of India, observes:—"I do not place much reliance on the testimony of the Coolies who have lately returned from Mauritius;" and adds, "I am not satisfied with the summary manner in which the examinations have been taken by the Chief Magistrate, who appears throughout in the character of a partizan arguing in favour of the Coolie trade." As to the general reluctance of the natives of India to leave their homes, the most conclusive testimony is borne to that fact by some of the highest officers of the Indian Government; and that the prohibitory law is not felt to trench on their rights or wishes is clear from the statement of the late Governor-general himself, who distinctly says, "I do not believe that this law is yet felt as pressing hardly on the rights of the natives of India;" and he farther observes, "It was upon no understood practice, and only through the busy intervention of an active agency, that the first emigrants were led to seek their fortunes in Mauritius." Thus, then, it appears to the Committee, that with but few exceptions, not only those who have returned to India from the Mauritius express no desire or intention to return thither, but the population generally have either no wish to leave India, or are opposed to it.

It is, however, believed by your Lordship that emigration from India to Mauritius may be so regulated as to prevent fraud, and punish injustice, and to make it advantageous to the Indian labourer to resort thither. The experience of the past would seem to prevent the indulgence of this hope. Lord Auckland in his minute of the 15th April, 1841, gives it as his opinion that " no strictness of regulation, and no vigilance on the part of the authorities, would immediately prevent the infliction of grievous oppressions and deceits upon large numbers of persons, helpless from their poverty, and from their utter ignorance and inexperience;" and that no dependence can be placed on the police is evident from what his lordship adds; namely, that " it is but too true that this branch of our service is most defective and ineffective, and the different experiments which have been tried for its reform, have ended in disappointment." And, as a practical measure, Lord Auckland would so far relax the prohibition, as to permit the " skilful artizan, or the man of calculating enterprise," to emigrate. Beyond this it does not appear that his lordship would feel disposed to go.

They are persuaded that even if your Lordship were able to secure the object contemplated by the regulations in British India, which the Committee believe to be impracticable, it would be impossible to secure justice to the labourers in the Mauritius. The want of laws to provide proper shelter for them on estates ; the want of hospitals under proper regulations and control in the various districts in which they might be located ; the want of a due proportion of the sexes, which has led to the most frightful demoralization among those already there ; the want of a due sense of moral obligation, so often and so shamefully manifested by the great body of the planters of that colony ; but, above all, the want of an intelligent, active, and truly independent magistracy, to administer with impartiality and firmness wholesome and just laws, lead the Committee but to one conclusion ; namely, that it is their duty respectfully to state to your Lordship, that they are entirely opposed to the revocation of the prohibitory law, and earnestly to entreat Her Majesty's Government to withdraw the proposed measure.

Signed on behalf of the Committee,

J. H. TREDGOLD,
Secretary.

27, *New Broad Street, London,*
Feb. 28, 1842.

PETITION TO THE HOUSE OF COMMONS.

The humble Petition of the Committee of the British and Foreign Anti-Slavery Society.

SHEWETH,

That your petitioners respectfully call the attention of your Honourable House, to the proposed relaxation of the law prohibiting the exportation of labourers from British India, so far as the same affects Mauritius, a measure similar to that which your honourable House decidedly negatived in the session of 1840.

Your petitioners would remind your honourable House of the dreadful mortality which up to the period of its prohibition had marked the emigration of Coolies to that island, a mortality which it is stated was equal, in Port Louis, to from eight to nine per cent., and in the country, to from ten to eleven per cent., per annum; and to the disgraceful frauds which had been practised on a multitude of ignorant and helpless people.

Your petitioners would also call your attention to the frightful demoralization which has resulted from the introduction of a vast number of males into that colony, and from the opposition which appears to have been given to their religious instruction.

Your petitioners would further bring under the consideration of your honourable House the recorded opinion of the late Governor-General of India, that no regulations, however stringent, and no watchfulness on the part of the authorities, however vigilant, can prevent oppressions and deceits from being practised on the labourers, who may be induced to emigrate to Mauritius.

Your petitioners would also call your attention to the general state of the laws, and the administration of justice, in the Mauritius, as affording no guarantee of fair and honourable treatment to immigrants on that island.

For these reasons among others, your petitioners entreat your honourable House not to sanction the revocation of said prohibitory law, which they believe to be both wise and humane, and absolutely necessary to protect the Indian labourers from the recurrence of those evils, which the friends of humanity, the government, and the legislature, have had such just cause to deplore and condemn.

And your Petitioners, &c.

Signed on behalf of the Committee,

J. H. TREDGOLD.

27, *New Broad Street, London,*
   Feb. 28, 1842.

INDEX.

J. Haddon, Printer, Castle Street, Finsbury.

The following important ANTI-SLAVERY PUBLICATIONS *are now on sale:—Subscribers to the Society are entitled to have them at a reduction of twenty-five per cent. under the prices annexed.*

PROCEEDINGS OF THE ANTI-SLAVERY CONVENTION, held in London in June 1840. One volume 8vo, price fourteen shillings.

"We dismiss the volume with our heartiest commendation; of the interest and importance of its contents we cannot speak too highly. The extensive circulation of such a work, while favourable to the immediate object of the convention, cannot fail to strengthen the benevolent affections of our nature, and to cherish a spirit of enlarged, singleminded, and active philanthropy."—*Eclectic.*

"The Anti-slavery public are laid under deep obligations by the care and industry which have been bestowed upon this report, which appears to be full and faithful, and is elegantly printed. It is a monument of benevolent feeling."—*Patriot.* "The work is one of thrilling interest, and will be read with eagerness by every friend of human liberty and human happiness. No man interested in the question of slavery ought to be without it—and we may add no man who has it and reads it can be otherwise than interested."—*Nonconformist.* "The *Proceedings of the General Anti-Slavery Convention* is a bulky octavo of nearly six hundred pages, containing a full report of the sittings and subjects discussed at the meeting held in London last summer."—*Colonial Gazette.* "This volume contains a very full and faithful record of the proceedings; we regard it as a volume which will possess increasing interest for centuries to come."—*Christian Examiner.*

INDIA. SLAVERY AND THE SLAVE-TRADE IN BRITISH INDIA with notices of the existence of these evils in Ceylon, Malacca, Penang, and Singapore, from official documents. Price One Shilling.

Showing the extent of slavery in British India; the laws which regulate it; the present condition of the slave-population; the external and internal slave trade; and the proceedings in Great Britain and India relative thereto.

"This pamphlet contains a collection of facts, proving the existence of the evil to an enormous excess in India."—*East India Telegraph.*

A BRIEF VIEW OF SLAVERY, being the substance of the above. Price Five Shillings per hundred.

INDIA. SLAVERY IN INDIA, by Professor William Adam, of Cambridge, Massachusetts, United States. Second Edition. Price Twopence.

The author of this pamphlet having resided in India for many years, his statements may be fully depended upon, as to the extent of slavery in India.

AMERICA. SLAVERY AND THE INTERNAL SLAVE-TRADE IN THE UNITED STATES OF NORTH AMERICA; being replies to queries, &c. In one vol. 8vo. Price Four Shillings.

"A more complete portraiture of slavery than has ever before appeared. The caution, fidelity, and temper with which it is executed, are altogether admirable. It is better fitted than any volume which has yet issued from the press, to convey to English readers a knowledge of the entire subject, and should be perused by all who wish to become thoroughly acquainted with it."—*Eclectic.* "We have here a document of great interest, and unquestionable value—an unimpeachable testimony as to the real state of things in the Union, as far as slavery and the internal slave trade are concerned."—*Times.* "A work of fearful interest and importance. That no doubt may be entertained of its authenticity, we would remind the reader that they rest upon the exclusive authority of Americans themselves."—*Churchman's Monthly Review.* "This volume may be received as an arbitrator, to end the strife; for its allegations, although put forth by abolitionists, are made upon authorities which Southerners can never contradict."—*Anti-Slavery Reporter.*

AMERICA. THE AMERICAN CHURCHES THE BULWARKS OF AMERICAN SLAVERY. Second Edition. Price One Shilling.

This pamphlet contains most indisputable evidence as to the extent to which most of the churches in America are involved in the guilt of supporting the slave system, and is published with a view to make the British Christian public acquainted with the real state of the case.

THE CONDITION OF THE FREE PEOPLE OF COLOUR IN THE UNITED STATES OF AMERICA. Price Threepence.

Reprinted from the "Anti-Slavery Examiner," published at New York in 1839. It shows the degrading position in which people of colour are placed in the *free* states of America.

AMERICA. A LETTER TO THE CLERGY OF VARIOUS DE-NOMINATIONS, and to the Slave-holding Planters in the southern parts of the United States of America. By Thomas Clarkson. Price One Shilling.

CUBA. SLAVERY IN CUBA. An address presented to the General Anti-Slavery Convention. By R. R. Madden, Esq., M.D. Price Sixpence.

A concise statement of the actual state of Slavery in Cuba, and the administration of Spanish law in that colony.